I0418362

FOUNTAINS OF WAYNE

ALSO AVAILABLE

Brainiac by Justin Vellucci

De La Soul by Dave Heaton

AFI by Andi Coulter

FOUNTAINS OF WAYNE

Fiona McQuarrie

J-Card Press

COPYRIGHT © 2025 BY FIONA McQUARRIE

All rights reserved. This book or any portion thereof may not be reproduced or used in any manner whatsoever without the express written permission of the publisher except for the use of brief quotations in a book review.

ISBN: 979-8-9891947-8-0 (print)
ISBN: 979-8-9891947-9-7 (ebook)

Library of Congress Control Number: 2024953066

J-Card Press
460 Center Street #6578
Moraga, California 94570

Interior design by Seth Shapiro
Photo retouching by Beth McKenzie

www.jcardpress.com

For Tom—
I'd never make it through without you around.

I think we'll be able to take our albums off the shelf in ten years and still like them.

—Adam Schlesinger, 2004

CONTENTS

INTRODUCTION: HERE WE ARE AT LAST

F ountains of Wayne's career has spanned close to three decades, filled with outstanding albums and peerless songwriting. After the band released its last album in 2011, there was always the hope that even as its four members went in different musical directions, they might eventually be inclined to work together again. Adam Schlesinger's death in 2020 ended that possibility, but the posthumous tributes to him and the group demonstrated just how well loved Fountains of Wayne were, and still are.

The Fountains' recording career coincided with a time of massive evolution in the music industry. The band started out with Chris Collingwood and Adam Schlesinger playing cover tunes in bands at college, and then proceeded through the boom of small independent labels, vinyl being replaced by CDs, the World Wide Web, online file sharing, Myspace, Napster, MTV, iTunes, Amazon, Bandcamp, and media corporatization and concentration. The Fountains' story is its own unique story, but those changes affected hundreds, if not thousands, of artists during the same era. One can only wonder if Fountains of Wayne's career trajectory would have been different in a more predictable or stable environment.

Some have dismissed the Fountains as one-hit wonders, which, thanks to "Stacy's Mom," they technically are (although, as Alicia "I Love the Nightlife" Bridges once said, to have even one hit is a wonder). "Stacy's Mom" was my own gateway into Fountains of Wayne, and I know I'm not the only person to have had that experience. I discovered the song through the regular airings of its video on MuchMusic (the Canadian equivalent of MTV). I wasn't part of the demographic that the video was aimed at, and by then I was also pretty much done with music videos that were more about scantily clad girls than about the music, or the musicians making the music. However, the "Stacy's Mom" video was different. For one thing, the song itself was tremendous; it didn't really need Rachel Hunter in various stages of undress to sell it. But the video managed to hit all the visual clichés of that genre of music video while simultaneously casting a cynical side-eye at their ridiculousness. I got the subversion and I appreciated it, which led me to acquire the album that included "Stacy's Mom," and that, in turn, led me into the rest of the band's catalogue.

When I've told people that I'm writing a book about Fountains of Wayne, the responses fall into one of two categories: "Who?" or "Oh, yeah, 'Stacy's Mom,'" accompanied by a dismissive sneer. I've also started to notice during my record store visits that it's very rare to actually see a Fountains of Wayne album or single. Yes, I know a lot of that material is online, but with the infinite amount of music that can be streamed—and with that lack of visibility in stores—the chances of new listeners randomly encountering Fountains of Wayne are minimal.

This is why the Fountains of Wayne story is important. This band should be remembered, and they should be remembered for so much more than "Stacy's Mom." With their unassuming stage presence—although they could rock as hard as any of their peers—and their songs about drudge jobs, romantic heartbreak, and not being the coolest one in the room, they gave a voice to bored corporate drones trapped in cubicle farms, and to music lovers fed up with bombastic swagger and aural overkill. Their music was both ordinary and extraordinary: a contrast that is difficult to successfully balance, but they did it. Even at the height of their popularity, Fountains of Wayne never lost their ability to connect with people living regular lives.

It may have been inevitable that the different working methods of the band's two songwriters would eventually lead to Fountains of Wayne drifting apart. But the same thing happened to them that happens to any long-time group of friends or coworkers: people evolve and change. During their time together, the members of Fountains of Wayne grew from young men in their late twenties into mature adults in their early forties, with increasingly different interests and priorities. Those changes also contributed to them gradually going off to do their own individual things. But in retrospect, Fountains of Wayne's music holds up much better than many acts who outsold them in their heyday—and that is another reason why their story deserves more attention. This book tells that story.

1. TWO OF A KIND

Fountains of Wayne grew out of the collaboration between Adam Schlesinger and Chris Collingwood, so the story of the band has to start with their stories. They were born just a few weeks apart from each other in October 1967, at the tail end of the Summer of Love—a musical and cultural era that would influence the music they eventually made together—and they grew up in towns a few hours' drive apart in the northeastern US.

Adam was born in New York City. His grandfather's family ran a company that presented national tours of Broadway musicals; his mother, Bobbi, was an arts publicist, and his father, Steve, an administrator at a granting foundation, also played clarinet. Adam and his younger sister, Laurie, grew up in a lively, creative Manhattan household, and he showed very early signs of the inquisitive and articulate person he would become. Jeremy Freeman, one of his best friends since early childhood, remembered an event during a seaside vacation that their families took together, when he was two years old and Adam was three. Jeremy was placed in a red toy wagon that Adam decided to pull, and Jeremy, as yet unable to speak, resisted by biting him. Adam, shocked, looked at his mother and said, "But I am not something to eat."

When Adam was five, his family moved from Manhattan to Montclair, a township in northern New Jersey. He later characterized Montclair as having "a strange and complicated relationship with New York City." It was close enough to the Big Apple for easy access to all its wonders but rooted in the distinctive working-class suburban ethos of the Garden State. After Adam started school, he became involved in all sorts of activities. In middle school and high school, he competed in spelling bees, played baseball, was a member of the student council, drew pictures, and painted. And he loved music. "I had been given a bunch of Beatles records by my aunt when I was about three," he recalled, "and that was pretty much the extent of my record collection until I was probably seven or eight, and then I discovered that there were other musicians in the world."

Adam's first formal musical training was in jazz piano. "In the fifth grade there was always a piano in the classroom," his friend Neal Robinson remembered, "and in between classes he wrote little songs. If ever there was an instrument around, he would play it." One of his middle school teachers later recalled him always having a guitar in his hand as he roamed the school halls. Adam performed in some of the musicals that were staged at school, including playing young Winthrop Paroo in *The Music Man*: a role Chris would also play in his own school's production of the same musical. In high school, Adam played bass and keyboards in a band called Prufrock that performed several shows on the lawn of the Montclair Public Library. Prufrock's biggest event was a library-sponsored free festival that also featured hard-core punk band Mechanized Death, which, the local newspaper dryly noted, "has a sound that is quite different from

Prufrock's."

Chris grew up in Sellersville, Pennsylvania, a town in a rural area near Philadelphia. His family briefly lived in Amity Gardens, a residential development in nearby Douglassville, before moving to Sellersville. His father, David, worked as a pharmaceutical company executive and his mother, Shirley, taught public school. It wasn't a region with a particularly lively music scene; the most notable musician from the area was Daryl Hall of Hall & Oates, who was born in Pottstown, about thirty miles west of Sellersville.

Sellersville was a small agrarian community, but it was close enough to larger cities that many of its residents commuted to jobs elsewhere. Chris had fond memories of going to agricultural fairs, visiting his grandparents' farm, and participating in sports with his brother William, but he also felt there were "conflicting value systems between me and my family." He acknowledged the value of hard work in a farming community, but he resisted "hard work for very little purpose—getting up at the crack of dawn and hammering stakes and digging holes, moving rocks around, and my reaction to that was that it was always kind of misdirected energy and kind of a waste of time."

When Chris was five years old, he had a little blue transistor radio at his grandmother's house in Douglassville. He listened with fascination to Top 40 hits such as the Looking Glass's "Brandy" and the Raspberries's "Go All the Way." "That's probably my earliest memory of being transfixed by music," he later wrote. "In the way children understand these things, I guess I thought it was magic." Then, like so many other kids his age, he discovered more enduring bands like the Beatles, the Kinks, the Hollies, and the Zombies—although he didn't own a lot of albums. The first two things his parents allowed him to buy for himself were Meat Loaf's *Bat Out of Hell* and the Cars' self-titled debut album. Later, his father disapproved of his buying Tom Petty's debut album, because it had twelve tracks on it and Chris had only heard "Breakdown."

Chris spent his high school years at the Hill School, a private boys-only boarding school in Pottstown whose alumni included numerous high-profile politicians, scientists, intellectuals, and diplomats. He recalled the place as "really conservative—it wasn't complete torture, but I didn't really fit the mold." During tenth grade he started playing guitar. Due to new music not being "cool" among his classmates, he became familiar with older acts such as the Doors and the Moody Blues, and with sixties pop in general. But, he later said, "I was a geek, I was a bookworm, and I was pretty afraid to do anything wild."

Adam's and Chris's paths first crossed in 1985, at Williams College in northwestern Massachusetts. After graduating from high school in summer that year, both Adam and Chris started classes at Williams in the fall. Williams was, and is, a small highly ranked undergraduate liberal arts college, with extensive academic and extracurricular opportunities for its students, including its own arts museum, astronomical observatory, and radio station. Chris was a top student at his high school, but he went to college mostly because, well, that's what graduates of prestigious prep schools were expected to do. "I really don't know how I ended up at college. I don't know what the hell I was thinking. It was just a really silly thing to be there, and I was too immature to even appreciate it for what it was." Adam's father was a Williams alumnus, and as an avid student, Adam looked forward to higher education. He quickly established himself at Williams as the leader of the Rhythm Method, a popular band that played cover versions of eighties songs at campus parties.

Williams had a total enrollment of only two thousand students, so it was perhaps inevitable that the two music lovers would eventually meet. Adam and Chris first encountered each other one afternoon on the balcony that ran across the back of the dormitory buildings where they lived. The story they both told numerous times was that Adam was sitting at one end of the balcony playing an R.E.M. song on his guitar, and Chris, playing his own guitar at the other end of the balcony, took it upon himself to come over and tell Adam that he was playing the wrong chords. From that awkward beginning, though, they discovered their mutual appreciation of the same kinds of music and started getting together regularly to jam and play albums, and to talk about songs and bands that they loved.

At that point in the mid-eighties, Chris later recalled, he was enchanted by artists with a strong melodic sound and emotional, wistful lyrics—the Plimsouls, the Go-Betweens, Echo and the Bunnymen, Orange Juice, the Blue Nile, Billy Bragg, the Smiths. In addition to those bands, Adam was also a fan of the Police, XTC, and the Pretenders. "We had different records in our collections," Adam said, "but we also traded a lot." The band whose music influenced Chris the most, though, was Aztec Camera. "[Their music was] idealist, romantic, and downright poetic. The words weren't just taking up space. Even heady abstractions seemed to resonate with some strange authority." The music he was falling in love with made him feel "engaged with pop songs on a level I hadn't before. They could ponder uncertainties and paint pictures and hint at complex emotions without literalism or sappiness."

The songs that Chris and Adam admired were incorporated into the sets of the band that they started. It was a group with rotating membership—Adam described it as "more like a club than a functioning band"—and a new name every few weeks. Among the names that the band went through were Woolly Mammoth, Are You My Mother, Green Light Go, and Three People Standing Side by Side Have a Wingspan of Over 12 Feet. Chris's explanation for the name changes was, "If people saw us once, if we had the same name, they'd never come back."

Adam also played piano with the Williams jazz ensemble, and Chris became the co-host of a regular on-campus "open mic" night, during which he would occasionally perform a cover version of a song that he liked. As they worked individually and together on playing other artists' songs, they also gradually started writing music together, and occasionally would try out a new number at a live gig. However, both were honest in admitting that their own songs were not popular. Their college audiences wanted to hear the hits and were not tremendously receptive when Adam or Chris would slip an original composition into the set list.

One of Adam and Chris's more notable musical ventures was a band named the Price Choppers, for which they recruited economics student Phil Harris on bass and fine arts student Jeff Perrott on drums. The group wrote and played music for the 1987 edition of the Freshman Revue, an event started in the late forties by Stephen Sondheim when he was a Williams student, and held on campus every fall. The Williams student newspaper described the 1987 show as "a fast-paced blend of comedy, music and dance that poignantly explored the anxieties and hopes of college life," with songs satirizing conflicts between roommates, dining hall food, and the campus party scene.

Neither Adam nor Chris went to Williams with the goal of becoming a professional musician, but as they approached graduation, they began to consider whether that might be a possibility. Chris later said that he had wanted to be a rock singer since he was a kid. Adam's friend Jonathan Small was the son of film score composer Michael Small, and from watching the busy career of his friend's dad, Adam knew that it was possible to make a living by playing music. They both realized that it was a tough industry, with no guarantee of success. But, Chris recalled, "we spent a lot of time listening to records and saying to each other, 'This band made it. How hard can it be?'" Since neither of them had any firm post-graduation plans, they decided to at least give it a try.

2. THE UPS AND DOWNS, THE HIGHS AND LOWS

After graduating from Williams in 1989—Chris with a BA in psychology, Adam with a BA in English and philosophy—Chris moved to Boston, while Adam shuttled between Boston and New York City. Adam shared a place in New York with his friend Jonathan, and both Adam and Chris worked off-and-on day jobs. Adam was a legal transcriber for a while and spent some time at a PR firm that counted Sting among its clients, while Chris took a series of temporary jobs in computer programming.

Adam, Chris, and Jeff Perrott formed a band they named the Wallflowers, with Adam and Chris as the principal songwriters. Adam and Chris mostly wrote independently and brought their songs to each other at various stages of completion. Each one would usually make any adjustments that the other suggested, although often the song remained almost entirely as its creator presented it. They decided early on that every original song they performed or recorded would be credited to both of them, even if either Adam or Chris was largely responsible for it. Adam explained that this was "so we wouldn't be arguing about it and fighting about money and stuff."

Even at this embryonic stage of their musical partnership, they had different ways of approaching the process of songwriting. Adam was a quick writer, experimenting with different genres and lyrical ideas until something clicked, and structuring his writing schedule to keep himself on track and productive. Chris was less deadline driven, working on ideas as they arrived, and wasn't too bothered if a song didn't yet feel complete; he would wait until he hit on whatever was needed to finish it off. He characterized the contrast between their methods as "[Adam] writing songs built around phrases, and they're pretty linear. Mine tend to be less formulaic [and] more obtuse." Adam described their output during this period of creative development as either "abstract meditations on things, or trying to sound like the Kinks." A common element in both of their creative processes was a fascination with the songs of bands like the Kinks: songs that told small stories of individual events and lives while tapping into universally accessible themes—heartbreak, boredom, alienation, joy—set to irresistible melodic hooks and chord progressions.

After playing gigs in and around the northeastern US, the Wallflowers attracted the interest of Pipeline Records, a new independent label that was an offshoot of a record distribution company of the same name, based in Hicksville on New York's Long Island. Pipeline's only other artist at the time was a glam metal band named Valentine Saloon. In the fall of 1991 the Wallflowers signed to the label (minus Perrott, who had enrolled in a Master of Fine Arts program at Yale). But around the same time, Jakob Dylan, son of Bob, was fronting a band in California also named the Wallflowers. The younger Dylan got wind of the shared name, and, presumably having more financial resources to draw on than two indie musicians, offered Adam and Chris a payment—reportedly between $2,000 and $5,000—to change their band's name, so that his Wallflowers would be the only Wallflowers. They accepted the deal, and Adam and Chris's Wallflowers became Pinwheel (sometimes spelled Pinnwheel).

Adam and Chris had already recorded a demo of four of their songs. One of the cassettes of those demos—sent out while Pinwheel was still the Wallflowers—made its way to Michael Krumper. Krumper recalled that at the time he was "managing Robyn Hitchcock and Marshall Crenshaw, two other artists making music that was too smart for their own good." He decided to take on Pinwheel as a management client, because he felt their work had potential. He described them as "overeducated, precocious, and winning," and was particularly impressed with Adam's business sense and familiarity with the workings of the industry.

When Pinwheel needed a guitarist, Adam decided to search the "Musicians Wanted" classified ads in the *Village Voice*, New York City's "alternative" weekly newspaper. He came across an ad from a guitarist looking for collaborators that mentioned Prefab Sprout and the Go-Betweens as influences. As these were two of Adam and Chris's favorite bands, Adam contacted the ad's author, Andy Chase. They met in Chase's apartment—"our big business meeting," according to Chase, "we were in our early twenties"—and Adam admitted that he was actually looking for a guitarist for his own band. However, after Adam left, Andy's girlfriend Dominique Durand, who had been listening to their conversation from another room, told him, "That guy is cool. You should keep in touch with him." Chase had a small studio in NYC, so he invited Adam to come by and work on some songs. After hearing Durand sing, they decided that her smooth French-accented voice would be perfect for the music they were creating. The trio ended up recording demos of several songs in a style that a critic later called "infectiously bittersweet pop music" and dubbed themselves Ivy.

The entrepreneurial Adam also had several other irons in the fire. He was playing keyboards for live performances by The Red House, a New Jersey band that had recently released its first major-label album. When The Red House broke up, Adam, along with drummer Bob Nicol, joined Les Enfant Terribles, the backing band for singer/songwriter Rebecca Blasband. She was soon to become (in)famous as Becky on the first season of MTV's pioneering reality show *The Real World*. Adam could be glimpsed very briefly in one of the show's early episodes, playing backup guitar for Blasband at a live gig as she sang Pinwheel's "Half a Woman." Blasband and the group got as far as playing a few record company showcase gigs, but according to Nicol, "Becky took off for two months to California" and the band fell apart.

Pipeline put Pinwheel into the studio to record an album with a producer. The sessions were not productive; the band didn't get along with the producer, and the producer didn't get along with the band. A set of thirteen songs dubbed the "Pinwheel Sessions" or the "Pinwheel Demos" has surfaced on the internet; the source of the songs is not identified, but these may be the tracks that were intended for that album. The tracks were obviously recorded in a professional studio, and the relatively complete arrangements suggest they were more than songwriting demos or pre-production recordings.

The wordy, occasionally dense lyrics of the Pinwheel Sessions songs show the influences of Adam and Chris's beloved English bands and literary heroes. The song topics lean toward generic "love is complicated" territory. Most of these tracks wouldn't have sounded out of place on the college or alternative radio playlists of the era. That being said, they don't have a distinctive character or sound that would have gotten them noticed. For every standout track, such as the wistful "Bluer Than Blue" or the harmony-laden "Some Girls Tell Lies," there's a more generic number such as the lyric-heavy "Loveland" or "Holland Street." But even at this early stage, signs of Adam's and Chris's future directions as songwriters and musicians are starting to emerge. There's an underlying pop sensibility—informed by the sounds of the sixties and the seventies, but not slavishly copying them—and lush vocal arrangements, catchy chord sequences, and inventive melodies.

When Pinwheel's album was presented to Pipeline, the label refused to release it. To make the situation even worse, Pipeline also filed lawsuits against the band that essentially made it impossible for Chris and Adam to record or release anything else. This was a big blow to two young artists just trying to embark on their professional careers. "We couldn't get off the label and they wouldn't let us do anything or release our record or let us go work for anybody else. It was kind of a nightmare for two years," Adam recalled. "We were so depressed at that point. We felt, 'We're only 24 years old and we've totally fucked ourselves.'"

Krumper arranged an industry showcase gig for Pinwheel at New York's CBGB in 1993 and invited A&R representatives from several different labels, hoping to generate interest in the band. Instead, he witnessed most of the guests exiting the venue as soon as they could after Pinwheel's set. One of them told him that the band's sound was "too soft and edgeless." Not long after that, in the face of the lack of industry interest and the ongoing Pipeline lawsuit, Pinwheel called it quits.

Chris went back to Boston, where he continued to work as a computer programming temp at banks and colleges, even winning a few "Temp of the Month" awards. He formed a band named Mercy Buckets—its name a play on the French phrase *merci beaucoup* ["thank you very much"]—that covered Gram Parsons and Kris Kristofferson songs, because he "just didn't want to listen to rock music anymore." But temp work started to wear on him, especially as he saw his friends in the Boston and New York City music scenes leading more interesting lives than his.

Adam, in the meantime, developed yet another creative sideline: writing jingles for TV and radio commercials. A mutual friend referred him to Steven M. Gold, who ran a "jingle house" out of his NYC studio. Adam showed up at the studio with another friend, David Bar Katz, who was then part of the development team for *House of Buggin'*, a TV show commissioned by the Fox network and starring comedian/actor John Leguizamo. The three hit it off and began collaborating on music for the show; Adam subsequently worked with Gold on music for several commercials.

In 1994 Ivy, Adam's band with Andy Chase and Dominique Durand, were signed to Seed Records, an offshoot of Atlantic Records. While there was a long history of major record labels having multiple labels under their corporate umbrellas, Seed was just one example from that particular era of majors trying to piggyback on the burgeoning indie music scene by setting up faux-indie labels to sign quirky, individualistic bands. These labels had the benefit of corporate resources and backing, but the control of their major label parents included implicit expectations of mainstream success—with the incentive that if a band was successful enough, the corporate parent might move them onto one of its more established labels. Ivy's signing was initially hampered by complications around the Pipeline lawsuit, which might have restricted Adam's ability to enter into another music-related contract. But, as it happened, Pipeline went bankrupt and the Pinwheel-related lawsuit was finally dropped.

Adam then took his own step into the business side of the industry by starting the Scratchie Records label. The impetus for founding Scratchie was his childhood friend Jeremy Freeman, who wanted to license and distribute Jamaican dancehall records in the US. Freeman and Adam, along with James Iha and D'Arcy Wretzky from Smashing Pumpkins, and Wretzky's husband Kerry Brown, collectively came up with $50,000 to launch Scratchie, and Freeman took on the role of president. The label quickly expanded beyond album distribution into signing its own acts, starting with the hard-rock quartet Chainsaw Kittens.

Up in Boston, Chris kept plugging away at his own songwriting in between, and sometimes during, temp jobs. Eventually he gave Adam a call to get feedback on some of the songs he had been developing. Several long-distance conversations ensued, and they decided that they would try recording an album for Chris, with Adam as producer. Chris was persuaded to move to New York City, where he continued his computer-related temping career. Adam and Chris regularly socialized together at the WXOU Radio Bar, a friendly dive bar in the West Village located a few blocks from Adam's fifth-floor walk-up apartment. The bar was popular with many musicians who lived in the city, attracting all kinds of creative people seeking an amiable low-key place to hang out for an evening.

At the bar, Adam and Chris would amuse each other by writing jokey song titles on cocktail napkins, which they then passed back and forth, challenging each other to write songs using those titles. But that lighthearted entertainment sparked more serious discussions about their own musical direction. They knew they could work together, they had songs, and they were free of the Pipeline contract. So, they decided, rather than making an album featuring just Chris, they would make an album together.

3. WE GOT SOME BIG THINGS BREWING

A dam and Chris recorded demos of four of their newer songs—"Radiation Vibe," "Sink to the Bottom," "Joe Rey," and "She's Got a Problem"—and passed the cassette along to Krumper, who by now was working at Atlantic Records. He was impressed. As he remembered, "The lyrics channeled the banter I heard constantly come out of Adam's and Chris's mouths." At the time—late 1995—the singles charts included a broad range of genres: the hip-hop and soul mélange of TLC, the classic R&B of Mariah Carey duetting with Boyz II Men, the folky pop of Deep Blue Something, the club-influenced coolness of Everything but the Girl. Adam and Chris's music didn't sound like any of those artists, but the mixture of styles on the charts suggested there was an opportunity for acts with well-written songs that had something different to offer.

However, Adam and Chris's project needed a name, even though at that point the project consisted of just the two of them. The source of the Fountains of Wayne name was apparently Adam's mom. While driving on the highway through northern New Jersey she saw the store named Fountains of Wayne, and then suggested to Adam that the store's name would be a great band name. Fountains of Wayne was a landmark in the town of Wayne, northwest of Montclair; it sold not only fountains but also outdoor furniture, birdbaths, garden statues, and all kinds of yard decorations. But the store was truly legendary for its annual "Fabulous Christmas Spectacular," which had been running for more than two decades. Every year, starting in mid-November, a forty-foot-tall Santa Claus figure was installed in the outdoor parking lot, and the entire first floor of the store was stocked with Christmas ornaments and decorations. The second floor became a dizzying realm of animated dioramas depicting fantastical seasonal scenes, such as Santa swimming under the sea, Santa orbiting in outer space, Santa at the beach, and Santa's elves hammering away in their workshop. Every year several themed displays would reflect current events, such as a tribute to the US Armed Forces during the Iraq War. There was no admission charge to visit this holiday wonderland, so a trip to Fountains of Wayne at Christmas was a tradition for many families in the region.

Adam admitted to having some qualms about naming his and Chris's band "Fountains of Wayne." Chris was even less enthusiastic, and Krumper didn't like the name much either. But there certainly wouldn't be a Wallflowers-type problem with another band using the same name, and, as Krumper noted, the name was eminently Googleable—this becoming more of a consideration as the reach of the internet was expanding. So Fountains of Wayne it was, after a visit to the store to get the owner's approval. "He was worried at first that we were going to be heavy metal guys or gangsta rappers," Adam reported, "but he was OK with it after he met us."

With Steve Yegelwel taking the role of the group's A&R representative, Fountains of Wayne was signed to Atlantic in early 1996, joining Ivy on the label's roster of artists. The band was assigned to TAG Recordings, an Atlantic imprint which, like Ivy's label Seed, was designed to give the appearance of being an independent label. (Singer-songwriter Dan Bryk wryly described this era as "the major-label faux-indie-rock gold rush.") Fountains of Wayne was also listed on the roster of Adam's Scratchie label, which had struck a distribution deal with Mercury Records, but it was eventually decided that the Fountains of Wayne album would be jointly released by Scratchie and TAG, with Atlantic being responsible for distribution and promotion.

The band also aligned its business operations with another and perhaps more surprising partner: Q Prime Management, the music management company whose client roster included Metallica, Def Leppard, and Queensrÿche. Two smart-ass college graduates writing quirky pop songs who had yet to release an album seemed a somewhat unlikely fit with a company that primarily represented stadium-filling metal bands. But Q Prime was embarking on a strategy to broaden the scope of acts it represented; it had recently signed alterna-stars Smashing Pumpkins and Courtney Love and Hole. Fountains of Wayne also met Q Prime cofounder Peter Mensch's criteria for acts to be represented by the company: "No assholes, and at least one member who takes an interest in business." Cliff Burnstein, the company's other cofounder, said, "I just loved the songs, and Chris's voice. It's very hard to find a unique voice, and he has one. But essentially, good songs are what this business is based upon, and Fountains of Wayne have great songs."

"We were having fun, but at the same time we were

taking it seriously, and we felt like this new thing had potential," Adam later remembered. "It was a period where bands with guitars and a bit of a sense of humor were actually selling records, so it seemed plausible that something might happen." From Chris's perspective, "The idea that some giant company was going to give us more money than we'd ever seen to go around the world playing music seemed too good to be true."

Adam and Chris wrote most of the songs for the first Fountains album, according to Chris, "on some holiday weekend. We were the only two people left in New York, so we just got together and started writing again." They created "I've Got a Flair" and "You Curse at Girls" together—"in about five minutes, whatever came to mind," Adam recalled—while other tracks began as individual compositions that one of them hadn't gotten around to completing. This included "Sick Day," which, Adam said, "I had written, but I got lazy and didn't finish the lyrics, so [Chris] finished the lyrics." "Leave the Biker" came out of Adam and Chris speculating what would happen to mild-mannered guys like themselves if they visited the notoriously wild Hogs and Heifers bar in New York City, which at the time had ceilings and walls covered with bras donated by patrons, and bartenders dancing on its bar tops. That song was written, by Adam's estimate, in about as much time as it took to play it through.

"A lot of the songs were set in New York City," Chris explained much later, "because I had just moved there a few years earlier. There's a sense of wonderment, and taking in the city. Half of that record is fascination with seeing so many things, and the other half just reflects the exhaustion. Really, it was just a snapshot of what was going on at the time. I had a computer programming job that earned me a lot of money, and I was young and living in the city and drunk."

Adam and Chris decided to continue their practice of being jointly credited as writers on all of Fountains of Wayne's songs. In addition to avoiding the potential for disagreement over how to divide royalties—a more relevant issue now that Fountains of Wayne was signed to a record label—"We wanted the band to have an identity more than we each wanted to have an identity within the band," Adam said. "We liked the anonymity in sharing the credit. A band doesn't need to be dissected that way."

Adam and Chris went into Andy Chase's NYC studio, the Place, in January 1996 to record their album. The sessions went remarkably fast. In eight days, playing every instrument themselves except bass (played by their friend Danny Weinkauf), they had finished almost all the album tracks. The songs from the demo tape were recorded pretty much as they had sounded on that cassette. Only a short time in another New York studio, Greene St. Recording, was needed to polish things off in the spring.

Adam later observed, "Some bands have these careers that are thirty or forty years long, and they're playing these three or four songs that they wrote when they were in their teens or twenties that everyone still knows. So you spend an afternoon writing these songs as kids, then all these years later you're still playing it, trying to remember where it came from." It says something about the strength of that debut album that several of its tracks remained in the band's live sets for years.

Fountains of Wayne has its share of the sounds that characterized that musical era—thrashy guitars, relentlessly crashing drums, quiet-loud-quiet song structures. Adam said nearly a decade later that of all the Fountains' albums, the first had "the most in common with what was going on at that exact moment, sort of an alternative-rock-pop album that wasn't that far removed from a lot of other records coming out that year." But it also demonstrated that Adam and Chris could write intriguing melodies, and could make something listenable and catchy out of the simplest lyrics or chords. Adam recalled that "consciously, we toughened up a bit when we were writing for the album, but the basic style is still there—writing on acoustic guitar, keeping the song simple, and concentrating on the melody and the lyrics."

Collectively, the album's tracks also demonstrated Adam and Chris' ability to convincingly portray a range of emotions and situations. Some of the songs were clearly rooted in the experiences of twenty-somethings trying to make their way in the big city—not surprisingly, given that's what Adam and Chris themselves were doing at the time. But their writing also touched on themes that pretty much any listener could relate to. The bored office worker of "Sick Day" "*crawling to work six feet under/And the day has barely begun*" is looking forward to giving herself a day off. The troubled friend of "She's Got a Problem" is "*a danger to herself/And I'm worried about her health*." The eccentric co-worker of "Joe Rey" (based on someone Chris actually worked with) "*smokes at three/barks like a pigeon/and watches TV*." The resilient protagonist of "Barbara H." who "*knows it doesn't matter at all*" was Chris's girlfriend Linda Stevenson; they met while they were both working temp jobs at the same company. "We met over the water cooler. I had an office, it had a water cooler in it, and I saw everybody, because people came into my office all day long." The song was written about her complete indifference to rock music, "including my own."

Fountains of Wayne was released in October 1996, amid a slew of publicity. The band actually played a launch event at Hogs and Heifers, and of course that set included "Leave the Biker." The first single was Chris's "Radiation Vibe," which Adam admiringly described as "one of the best songs ever, and it doesn't make any fucking sense. That's part of what I love about it. It's sort of anthemic, but when you stop to think about what you're saying, it's hilarious."

Ira Robbins, writing in *Rolling Stone*, praised the album as "a winning blast of power pop with textures that range from noisy guitar sizzle to wispy balladry," and noted the contrasts between Adam's and Chris's onstage personas: "Schlesinger is a casual overachiever who radiates exactly the opposite vibe. That goes double for Collingwood, whose laconic wryness makes him a perfect foil for the more upbeat and forthright Schlesinger." Lindsay Planer, in the *Charlotte Observer*, commented that the album was a welcome change from the angst-filled musical norm at the time, because it was a reminder that "pop music is supposed to be (gasp) fun." *Fountains of Wayne* was also welcomed by aficionados of power pop. Coincidentally, the same year Rhino Records released its three-CD *Poptopia!* compilation, which indicated the ongoing interest in this often underappreciated musical genre. Indeed, one review of *Poptopia!* observed that "the time may be right to hear [these songs] again, as the music begins lightening after years of downbeat rock, and sharp new bands like Fountains of Wayne inject new energy into the style."

The Fountains weren't single-handedly reviving power pop. Other relative newcomers such as Jason Falkner (whose album *Author Unknown* was praised by Adam and Chris) were also making a name for themselves as proponents of the genre. And there was definitely an audience looking for what one guide to the genre characterized as "an energetic interpretation of pop rock, based in equal parts on melodic hooks and killer instinct." Even the most devoted power pop aficionados would admit that the boundaries of the genre are fluid—certainly a Fountains track such as "Radiation Vibe" or "Sink to the Bottom" owed as much to guitar-driven grunge as it did to any other Top 40 musical style—but if the label of power pop made more people pay attention to the Fountains' music, no one was going to object too strongly.

"The best thing about [the album] for us," Adam said, "was just that it was so depressing, all the stuff that happened to us before, and we really felt like it was just such a waste, because we knew that we had something good going on. All our friends were always like, you know, why'd you guys stop playing together? And to be able to go in and do something, and especially to write new songs and not just be rehashing these same songs that have been kicking around for four or five years at that point—it was so refreshing."

An attempt to gain broad appeal for the album was made by releasing a music video for "Radiation Vibe." Directed by Clark Eddy, it featured nihilistic imagery like tapping feet next to feet nailed to the floor, interspersed with black-and-white shots of a character resembling *Twilight Zone* host Rod Serling and a strange young girl in a narrow hallway. Adam and Chris appeared in thrift-store outfits, miming the song and peering into the camera at odd angles. "We didn't really understand [the director's] video treatment," Adam said, "but we just thought, 'Let's trust him, he has stuff on MTV.' That was a time when MTV had an enormous amount of power to break a band. If we had made a bright, sunny, fun video for that song, our entire career could have started off on a much bigger level. Instead, we made this weird, dark, creepy video that had some kind of *Twilight Zone* elements that no one got except the director. It got some token MTV play, and that was it." Chris Applebaum directed a subsequent video, for "Sink to the Bottom"; while this was slightly more upbeat, with pastel color-saturated scenes of the band playing, it also featured what were rapidly becoming clichés of the era, such as surrealistic scenarios (the band members seated in chairs on a street and dangling fishing lines into a grotty urban sewer) and unsettling-looking characters wandering in and out of the action. That video went largely unnoticed too.

Although the songs on *Fountains of Wayne* definitely had a harder edge than the songs on the Pinwheel demos, Adam and Chris were very clear that they were not trying to follow trends—even when they had been told by A&R representatives that while the reps personally loved the band's music, their corporate mandate was to find the next Pearl Jam. Chris frequently expressed disdain for grunge music. "Those bands can't write songs, so they get over by jamming on some chord progression and going 'Uhhh . . .' until it sounds right to them."

The press release that accompanied *Fountains of Wayne* cleverly conveyed the message that the band's music had elements of current trends but definitely could not be categorized into any of them. It charmingly described the album as "combin[ing] soaring harmonies with sludge-filled guitars, clever wordplay with juvenile private jokes, [and] innovative arrangements with shameless rock clichés." (Ken

Weinstein, who became the band's longtime publicist, later revealed that Adam wrote many of the Fountains' press releases himself.) But the photo on the album's cover drew more attention than anyone had expected. The striking image of a young boy wearing a makeshift superhero outfit, standing outdoors and ready to take to the sky with a rabbit tucked under his arm, was by UK photographer Nick Waplington; it came from a series of photos Waplington took throughout the eighties on a UK housing estate. It was certainly eye-catching, which became even more apparent when Adam and Chris discovered that the photo had been used for another album cover: *Plastic Jewels* by the UK band Flamingoes. "He [Waplington] was directly asked by us if he had licensed it to anyone else, and he said no," Chris complained. Even more concerning was that with the alphabetical closeness of the bands' names, the two albums could end up next to each other in the *F* section at a record store, potentially confusing buyers. An alternate cover for *Fountains of Wayne*—a white sleeve with three still-life images from the band's videos placed in a band across the center—was used in some regions outside the US and the UK, but the picture of the boy and his rabbit was by far the most widely recognized cover for the album.

Adam and Chris's self-sufficiency gave them a lot of latitude in recording, but posed something of a problem for touring, since they could not perform all the instruments on the album's songs by themselves. Thus, they set out to recruit two other members for the Fountains, which is when guitarist Jody Porter and drummer Brian Young entered the picture. Jody, from Charleston, South Carolina, had played music from a very early age. Although he received a drum kit on his fourth birthday and a ukulele on his fifth birthday, it was the guitar he got for his seventh birthday that won him over. "I gave up drums for guitar because I like notes more than rhythm," he explained. "People ask why I chose to be a guitarist. The answer is simple. In the end, the guitar chose me." He also soaked up music from his father's LP collection, particularly enjoying the Rolling Stones and the Who.

Jody's first band was a "rootsy" combo called the Westwinds, but it was his second band, Foreign Aid, that made him locally renowned as a guitarist, even as a preteen. His school friend Shepard Fairey—later to become famous as the designer of the Barack Obama "Hope" campaign poster—recalled Jody and Foreign Aid "ripping through Hendrix, Stones, and Led Zeppelin covers at our local playground dance." However, all the band members were under twenty-one years old, which meant they had trouble getting gigs; most of the live music venues in the region were licensed and did not allow minors on the premises. Jody started writing his own songs while in Foreign Aid, and in later bands, including the Waltons and the Fields, he contributed most of the original numbers to their sets.

After turning nineteen, Jody moved to New York, where he met singer-songwriter Britta Phillips. They formed the band The Belltower, which also included Weinkauf, but in 1990, frustrated with what they perceived as the lack of opportunities in the US for genuinely independent bands, they moved to the UK. "People just box themselves into something that has been done fifty million times before," Phillips told an interviewer. "In the States, if you can play decently, it doesn't matter what creativity you put in." The Belltower released several well-received UK singles and EPs, followed by the album *Popdropper*, after which Phillips and

Porter returned to the US. The Belltower were signed to Scratchie and released a single, with Adam helping out on bass for some live dates. But Porter and Phillips' marriage disintegrated, which also meant the end of the band.

Adam suggested to Jody that he consider joining the Fountains, and Chris came to one of the last gigs by The Belltower so that he could see Jody play. "I thought, 'Who is that asshole?' And it was Chris," Jody later remembered with a laugh. "At the time, I was like, this guy's got an edge to him, and I felt like I was being judged by one of my peers that I didn't even put on the guest list." Despite that initial first impression, both Adam and Chris wanted Jody as the band's guitarist, and he agreed to join the Fountains.

Brian was originally from Pittsburgh and started playing drums as a high school student in Arizona, where he sat in with bar bands that covered country and R&B tunes. After studying at a music school in Los Angeles, he built a varied musical résumé, including playing in pit bands for touring shows and backing Japanese singer Junko Yagami. In 1994 he became part of the Seattle-based Posies, touring with them and appearing in Burt Bacharach's backing band in the first Austin Powers film. However, the Posies decided to take a break after their record label dropped them, and Brian then heard about the Fountains of Wayne opportunity through a friend who knew Adam. He auditioned for Adam and Chris, and impressed them by nailing the tricky rhythm patterns of Steve Miller's "Swingtown," after which he was hired. He became the last addition to the band, formally signing up the day before the "Radiation Vibe" video was filmed.

During this period, one of Adam's other projects suddenly became very prominent. As part of Ivy's contract,

Adam was signed as a writer to a music publishing company, and his contacts there let him know about a movie whose producers were looking for a song. The movie was the fictional story of a one-hit-wonder band in the sixties, and the producers wanted a song that would feature in the film as the hit by the Wonders. "They heard about this movie that was happening," Adam recounted, "and they said, 'You should take a crack at this. This is up your alley.'"

The title given to the prospective songwriters, and the title of the film, was "That Thing You Do!" Adam was somewhat puzzled as to what the "thing" was or what it did, but nonetheless he wrote three different sixties-style pop songs with that title, and recruited his and Chris's friend Mike Viola, from the band Candy Butchers, to sing them. Adam and Mike demoed all three songs with Andy Chase producing, then played the songs for several friends; they went ahead with the one that got the best reaction. When recording it onto a cassette, they added a subtle wobbly, scratchy tone to make it sound like a sixties single on vinyl. Adam and Mike submitted the tape to the film's producers under the name Scientist Alexis.

After several months of not hearing anything other than "We like it" and "Your song is still in the running," the producers chose their song—apparently out of more than three hundred submissions—to be the song in the film. (One of the other entries, "Little Wild One" by the Gigolo Aunts, also ended up being used in the film, as a song that the Wonders play earlier in their career.) "It's crazy that Tom Hanks and Gary Goetzman, his partner, had the confidence to pull a song out of a pile and say, 'Yeah, we like this one,'" Adam remembered. "These guys based an entire movie around a song written by some kid who they never heard of." *That Thing You Do!*, the film, was released in October 1996.

The new four-piece Fountains played a few dates in late fall, including opening for the Lemonheads in New Jersey, and a gig at a club near Hartford, Connecticut, that, according to the local paper, drew "exactly zero people." In November, Chris and Linda got married. In December, Adam was nominated for a Golden Globe Award for Best Original Song, for "That Thing You Do!" The band finished the year with a show in Chicago, co-headlining with Chainsaw Kittens and another Scratchie Records act, Fulflej.

4. I'M ON MY WAY

Fountains of Wayne kicked off 1997 in a very big way for a very new band. After a live performance on *Late Night with Conan O'Brien*—a television show they would regularly appear on in the future—the group was booked as the opening act on the January leg of Smashing Pumpkins' Infinite Sadness tour. The tour's name had become somewhat poignant, since some of the tour dates were rescheduled from the summer of 1996, following the death of Pumpkins keyboard player Jonathan Melvoin and the departure of drummer Jimmy Chamberlin.

There was a certain synergy between the two bands' during this era. The Fountains' music was more thrashy than it would be later, and Smashing Pumpkins' sound was more melodic and pop-oriented than that of other bands categorized as "grunge"—and of course Adam and Chris were already friends with James Iha and D'Arcy Wretzky of the Pumpkins. Nonetheless, the tour was a big jump for the band. They had only played together for a relatively short time and now were performing for audiences in multi-thousand-seat arenas. The high-profile exposure was clearly part of what Jody later described as Q Prime "building the band from the ground up. Their other acts were already pretty well established."

Adam told an interviewer that they recognized most of the audience was there to see the headliners, and thus Fountains of Wayne generally took to the stage "with a certain sense of humility." As the openers, the audiences they played to, described by one reviewer as "small and subdued," but the band made the most of their nightly forty-five-minute set, throwing in the occasional cover version amid songs from their album. The tour also gave the Fountains the chance to learn, by watching the Pumpkins, how a top-level band went about its work. While Adam joked that his band "got the opening-band light setting of ON" in comparison to the headliners' elaborate stage effects, he also noted, more seriously, "You can tell that they've got it down to a science. I think they've been very smart with their careers. They've played the game well."

The Golden Globes ceremony happened while the Fountains were on the tour, and "That Thing You Do!" was beaten in its category by Andrew Lloyd Webber and Tim Rice's "You Must Love Me" from the film *Evita*. But in February, the Academy Award nominations were announced, and Adam was shocked to learn that he was one of the nominees in the Best Original Song category. He told a reporter that he first heard the news from his mom, who "was screaming into my answering machine at 8:30 a.m., and when they didn't cover my category [on the TV broadcast of the announcements], she phoned up the Associated Press. She's very resourceful."

This unusual level of public visibility brought attention to the band, especially as Adam was a newcomer to writing music for films, and thus was something of a novelty compared to the much more experienced nominees in the same category. But it also led to confusion. While Adam wrote "That Thing You Do!," it wasn't a Fountains song, and it wasn't the Fountains that played on the song. Reviewers frequently misidentified "That Thing You Do!" as a Fountains of Wayne song. Some audience members at Fountains gigs showed up expecting to hear it, and even shouted requests for it. "It got us a lot of attention," Chris said, "but it created a lot of misconceptions"—a situation that Adam found somewhat concerning. "Chris wrote more than half the album," he said, "and as the band gets better known, it gets hard because people know me, but he deserves just as much credit."

After the Smashing Pumpkins tour ended, Fountains of Wayne stepped into a whirlwind of club dates in February and March, including a jaunt to Europe, where they appeared on the French television show *NPA* and played shows in London and Amsterdam. Adam took a quick break to attend the Academy Awards ceremony in March—"It was a bit like a high school prom," he said, "except I didn't want to talk to anyone"—where "That Thing You Do!" lost again to Rice and Lloyd Webber's song. Then it was back to North America in April, and over to Europe again for almost all of the summer and fall. A show at the famous Stone Pony club in New Jersey was filmed for the HBO channel's concert series *Reverb*, and aired toward the end of the year, as well as being re-run multiple times later on.

The band appreciated the club shows as opportunities to play to smaller audiences that were there to see them, rather than being faced with audiences who politely tolerated them while waiting for the headliners. It was also gratifying that the Fountains' performances generally got positive reviews. "A shimmering exuberance bursts through in the music," said Jim Sullivan of the *Boston Globe*, "[and] their pure pop doesn't insult your intelligence." Sara Sherr in the *Philadelphia Inquirer* called the music "keyed-up guitar-based pop . . . nineties bubble grunge: hooky enough for power pop fans, and loud enough for their younger brothers." Another reviewer noted that "while the band did not possess an excessively energetic vivacity, the harmonious and humorous performance was just as entertaining as I had heard and anticipated." Some writers, however, praised the band's songs but were less than enthusiastic about their stage presence. A reviewer in the UK said, "If you took the Fountains of Wayne to the beach, they'd just complain about the broken glass. I have to confess I spent the last half-hour of the show dreaming of things to wake them up."

Touring was demanding and exhausting. Playing so many live shows helped hone the cohesion and power of the Fountains' live performances, and as Chris and Adam became more confident at introducing songs and bantering with the audience, the band began to develop features of their shows that would last throughout their career. The closing number of the set was usually "Radiation Vibe," and the band began extending it into an instrumental jam during which they played snippets of other artists' songs—Joe Walsh's "Life's Been Good," ZZ Top's "Sharp Dressed Man," Simon and Garfunkel's "The Only Living Boy in New York," whatever they felt like trying that night. But the grind of touring also took a physical toll. There was a near-disaster on the Pumpkins tour in wintry Sioux Falls, South Dakota, when Jody slipped on some ice and hurt his arm. Luckily, the accident happened on a day off between shows, and he was able to rest up and perform the following night. Then Chris's voice started to suffer—a generally favorable review of a New York City show in April noted that he sounded "frayed from touring"—and some shows in early May had to be postponed when he came down with laryngitis.

As Fountains of Wayne's founders and songwriters, Adam and Chris also handled most of the band's promotional duties. While all four band members participated in TV appearances and other events that required the full band, Adam and Chris were usually scheduled for the radio, newspaper, and magazine interviews to promote the album or to publicize upcoming live dates. Like many new bands, they were also expected to attend industry events and showcases, and to meet local media in the cities where they played. According to Jody, Adam took on the additional task of "micromanaging" the band's activities while on tour: "He may have gotten a few more gray hairs than the rest of us." Another part of the promotional strategy for the band was participating in the opportunities that were starting to emerge for online engagement with audiences through the World Wide Web. In March and April, the Fountains participated in chat sessions on SonicNet—a "bulletin board" site that was becoming an online hub for music fans—and they also had an email address on CompuServe, another site that hosted fan discussions.

These efforts were starting to pay off in terms of establishing the band's credibility and presence. In the summer, a recruiting ad for a UK record company was looking for new A&R reps "with the ears and the bit in between to sign acts like The Aloof and Fountains of Wayne." But it was still a lot of work.

Balancing promotional responsibilities and demands

with the daily routine of traveling and performing is a challenge even for experienced musicians—and as *Fountains of Wayne* continued to receive favorable reviews, that in turn generated expectations for a fast turnaround and even more success with a second album.

There is a saying in the music industry that artists have seven years to write their first album and seven months to write their second one. While the numbers may not always be that precise, the situation described by the saying is very real. An artist making their first album has had years to polish their craft, and they go into the studio with the very best of whatever they've created during that long period of development. Then, if they are lucky enough to have their music catch on, while they're being patted on the back for being successful, they're also being pushed to quickly produce something that's as good as, if not better than, what literally took years to write and refine. The "difficult second album" is not just a cliché. Sarah McLachlan, whose career arc overlapped with the Fountains', explained the experience this way: "Your first album is learning to write songs, the second record [is] about a lot of high pressure from the label to write singles."

Adam and Chris were something of an exception to the "seven years and seven months" saying, since they had already completed an unreleased album, and then written all new songs for the Fountains' debut album in not much more than a week. But they were only able to do that because they had already worked together for several years. They understood each other as songwriters, and they had the expertise to recognize potential song topics and then to create interesting songs. But now, Fountains of Wayne were in a position where many newly successful bands have suddenly found themselves: their time taken up with traveling, performing, promotion, and publicity, while also being expected to produce new music—*good* new music. This may have been less of a challenge for Adam, who was used to juggling multiple projects and commitments, and as a result was accustomed to generating musical ideas and writing songs relatively quickly. Chris's more impressionistic writing process, however, relied on him being able to work through ideas and sounds at his own pace. That thoughtful process didn't always fit well with a relentless schedule of plane-bus-hotel-venue-hotel-bus-plane. And since the two of them wrote songs almost completely independently of each other, the creative process was rarely sped up through collaboration.

A fall trip to Europe turned out to be more eventful than expected when, at a show in Germany, Chris decided to do a dramatic leap onstage, and fell hard enough to break two ribs and a knee. This led to Adam having to make a solo promotional appearance on Xfm radio in London, where he performed acoustic versions of the newly written "Utopia Parkway" and the "Radiation Vibe" B-side "Karpet King." When Fountains of Wayne returned from Europe in early October, Ivy's second album, *Apartment Life*, was released; Adam had worked on it in between Fountains tours, and it included guest appearances from Chris and Jody. Adam turned his attention to promoting that album and playing a few live shows with Ivy. But then the Fountains regrouped, and started putting together their second album.

5. SO NOW DO YOU WANT ME?

As 1998 dawned, Fountains of Wayne were negotiating the process of making of their second album without having had a substantial hit single from their debut album, despite it being critically praised and selling well. Just over 90,000 copies of *Fountains of Wayne* were purchased in the US, and there was increasing interest in the band's music in other parts of the world such as the UK and Japan. Four tracks from *Fountains of Wayne* had been released as singles: "Radiation Vibe," "Sink to the Bottom," "Survival Car," and "Barbara H." All four had received radio airplay, particularly on college and alternative stations, but none had made it onto the US singles charts. Adam later suggested that *Fountains of Wayne*'s sales could have been higher if the album had been stocked in more stores, particularly after album tracks started to be added to radio playlists. In the UK, the first three singles had scraped into the lower reaches of the Top 40, as did the one-off single "I Want an Alien for Christmas," a song by Adam that he had unsuccessfully pitched to Hanson for their holiday album *Snowed In*. Instead, the Fountains recorded the song themselves while on tour in the UK during the summer of 1997. Released for the seasonal market at the end of the year, "I Want an Alien for Christmas" got to #37 in the UK Top 40, the band's highest-charting single anywhere to date.

Both Adam and Chris had continued their activities outside the Fountains. Adam guested on albums by James Iha and by the Gigolo Aunts, and he was also starting to be sought out by managers and record labels as a songwriter for hire. He co-wrote two tracks on the debut album by Swirl 360, an act centered around Denny and Kenny Scott, two "tanned, handsome 28-year-old twin brothers." While the duo resisted the label "manufactured," their songwriters were given the mandate to "[write] a song that would go straight to the heart of every teenage girl you ever saw," which was certainly the sort of musical direction that Adam excelled at. Chris produced an EP for the NYC-based band Tryst, but he was also becoming part of the music community in Northampton, where he and his wife had moved. The Massachusetts town about three hours north of New York City was also where Jody was now living. "It was just sort of time for a change," he told the Northampton newspaper about the decision to relocate there. "When I was in school we used to come down here all the time to see shows."

The band's live appearances in 1998 were limited to a few summertime festivals, while they worked on the second album. They were also on the bill at a festival in early spring where they must have felt somewhat out of place alongside single-named post-grunge rockers Live, Silverchair, Fuel, Orgy, and Sponge. In the fall, the Fountains participated in "British Invasion Revisited," a multi-act extravaganza of artists playing their favorite sixties Brit tunes, and played at a benefit in Boston for the satirical publication the *Weekly Week* ("Boston's Only Redundant News Source for News").

Adam also played a few dates with Ivy in the early part of the year. He told a reporter that he intended to continue being part of both Ivy and Fountains of Wayne, because the bands were musically different. "The tendency is to put one thing under a microscope, after which you lose your sense of perspective of what's good and what's not. I find this way [being in two bands at once] I keep both things in perspective." But in the spring Adam found himself in an uncomfortable dilemma when Ivy was dropped by Atlantic Records, and Fountains of Wayne were still on the label. Ivy's *Apartment Life* had been well received by critics, and two of the album's songs were licensed for the soundtrack of the hit film *There's Something About Mary*, but the group and the label apparently had different ideas about Ivy's future potential. "There were mixed signals," Adam said. "In their minds, they were doing us a favor [by dropping the band], but in the end it's better for everybody." Ivy made the best of the situation by quickly signing to another label and remastering and reissuing the album.

Work on the new Fountains album was facilitated by Adam now being the co-owner, along with James Iha and Andy Chase, of Stratosphere Sound, a recording studio in New York City. Stratosphere was a continuation of Chase's the Place studio, where the Fountains had recorded their first album. After Chase parted ways with his business partners in the Place, Adam and James came in as new investors and helped redevelop and relocate the studio's facilities. Most of the Fountains' second album was recorded at Stratosphere, with some of it also created at Adam's NYC home studio, whimsically dubbed Room with a Jew. By now, Jody and Brian were full participants in the band, allowing the Fountains to expand and refine their sound. "We indulged our little whims, and decided that overdubbing wasn't such a crime," Chris explained.

"The first album," Chris told *Billboard*, "is sort of a statement of purpose. It's like, 'Here's what we are; here's what we do.' If you try to make it too complicated and too weird, it tends to muddle the vision. But once you've established that, I think it's a natural progression to do something a little more diverse." However, both Adam and Chris recognized, based on their experience with the first album, that the choice of album songs mattered. "Whatever you put on your record," Adam said, "you'd better love it, because you're going to be playing it an awful lot."

The songs they came up with for the second album were a varied lot. It was obvious that Adam and Chris were trying to move from the rougher sound of *Fountains of Wayne* into something more refined, without losing that album's sense of spontaneity and its shambolic energy. The album was also an opportunity for the Fountains to show that they could do more than just bash away at guitars and drums. There were gentle, if somewhat rueful, ballads—"Troubled Times," re-recorded from the Pinwheel demos, with its simple yet powerful vocal harmonies; "A Fine Day For a Parade," with its worried elderly woman who is "*racking [her] mind/ Alone in the night*"; and "Hat and Feet" depicting post-breakup angst as reducing the dumped lover to "*a spot on the sidewalk/a mark on the street*." Then there were the faster-paced numbers that put the "power" in "power pop," such as "Laser Show," "Go, Hippie," and "It Must Be Summer" which upended the idea of summer being fun: "*The streets are bare/I try your number/But you're just not there*." Adam and Chris were also further developing their ability to create realistic characters through their lyrics. The protagonist of

"Red Dragon Tattoo" is a goof, but he's an earnestly sweet goof who truly believes that a tattoo—one that "*isn't painted on*"—will win over the girl he wants to impress. The woman described in "Amity Gardens" has escaped one dodgy situation for another, but now is wise enough not to return; "*If you knew now what you knew then/You wouldn't want to go home.*"

Utopia Parkway, the album's title, was the title of the opening song—a portrait of an ambitious young man with big dreams—and a reflection of the album's theme of life in suburbia. Utopia Parkway was also the name of an actual street in the New York City borough of Queens, and the album's cover image was a photograph of the street sign, set in front of an optimistic blue sky. "For a long time," Adam said, "I think the experience of growing up outside a city was not considered a legitimate theme. But there's a lot to write about, a lot that people can relate to. The city nearby builds a mysterious restlessness in people, a lot of ambition." The imagery in the CD booklet showed the idealization of cars, and the roads built for them, not only as a way to get around but also as a symbol of wide-open potential and socio-economic mobility.

Work on the album was mostly concluded by the end of 1998. In January 1999 Adam married his girlfriend Kate Michel, whom he had first met at the WXOU Radio Bar. After they became a couple, she had accompanied the band on the Pumpkins tour and was also Adam's date for the Academy Awards. "You go into this bar," she mused, "and suddenly your whole life is changed." The wedding was featured in the *New York Times'* "Vows" section, which reported that "the bride [wore] a greenish-white leather Prada suit with a miniskirt and a smile as big as Julia Roberts's."

Utopia Parkway hit record store shelves in April 1999, preceded by the first single, "Denise," with a video directed by Tryan George. With its staccato chords and distorted vocals, "Denise" was one of the *Utopia Parkway* tracks that was more reminiscent of the *Fountains of Wayne* sound, and thus perhaps would catch the ear of listeners who had enjoyed that album. The video featured model Jolene Blalock (who later starred in the TV series *Star Trek: Enterprise*) as the titular object of desire, prancing around in a provocatively filmed car wash, while the band posed and played in plastic Devo-ish jumpsuits. Another acknowledgment of the internet's increasing importance to music promotion was that prior to the album's official release, some tracks were featured on an exclusive "fancast" on Trans World Entertainment's website, requiring fans to use RealPlayer to join in.

But the release of the "Denise" single sparked a conflict between the Fountains and Atlantic. During the *Utopia Parkway* sessions, the Fountains had recorded a laid-back cover of Britney Spears's "...Baby One More Time." When Atlantic found out about the cover, they wanted to release it as an extra track on the single. "Here we had spent so much time working on our songs," Adam said later, "and they wanted to release one we hadn't written. It was kind of hurtful and insulting." "We recorded it because we liked the song, not because we wanted to have a big dumb novelty hit," Chris said. "The clear message we got was 'If you put this as a track on a single, we're going to make it the single.' So we pulled it off the single." Radio shock jock Howard Stern somehow got a copy of "...Baby" and played it on his radio show. The track also ended up as a file posted online on Napster, and became a popular download on that site.

The reviews of *Utopia Parkway* consistently mentioned

the quality of Adam and Chris's songwriting. Jonathan Perry in the *Boston Globe* praised the album as "not only rich with wry, pungent detail, but one that also sketches a universal portrait of adolescent dreams and suburban malaise with deft, deceptively simple strokes of guitar and pen." Brian McCallum of the *Detroit Free Press* said that "nothing here matches the sheer power-pop ecstasy of 'Radiation Vibe' from the previous album, but this is nonetheless a dandy, with unblinking snapshots of young suburbia in all its Gap glory." "It's the kind of disc that could grow on fans of poppish-rock, not just ones who grew up in Connecticut," said expat East Coaster Nick Jezierny in the *El Paso Times*. Elton John sent the band a handwritten letter, telling them: "It's the finest pop album I've heard in a while."

Another sign of the band's popularity after *Utopia Parkway*'s release was at the store the band was named after. According to Don Winters, the owner of Fountains of Wayne, teenage girls were now coming into the store who weren't looking for lawn ornaments or holiday displays—they just wanted one of the store's business cards. "I guess it's flattering," said his son, Brian, "but it hasn't helped our business all that much. My demographics are families with kids who want deck chairs, not teenagers into the latest music." Nonetheless, Don observed, "It's something else seeing your name in Sam Goody's."

Some critics carped that the band was making fun of the people portrayed in *Utopia Parkway*'s songs, to which Adam responded, "We're not looking down on people—if anything, we've been trying to amuse ourselves, but not at someone else's expense. I don't think we're mean-spirited at all. We're just a pop band." Ken Weinstein later said that "Adam's songs were deeply heartfelt and often really twisted and funny. He spent a lot of time carving out characters and their lives so it actually would upset him that the funny overshadowed the compassion. He wanted people to dig more deeply into the stories he wrote." Chris said that he and Adam "made a definite effort that every song was not a stupid one-liner."

Chris and Adam had to point out in multiple interviews that neither of them had tattoos, owned a custom van, or went to laser shows at planetariums—although Chris did admit that the charming yet ominous "The Valley of Malls" was partially inspired by his own drives through the region around Northampton. If listeners or reviewers thought that singing about ordinary people and their lives meant that the band members themselves were geeks, or nerds, or dweebs, Adam's tactful response to that perception was "I'm not really offended by it, but it's kind of missing the point."

The release of *Utopia Parkway* also fueled some of the band's fans to engage in an exercise of "who wrote what," despite Adam's caveat that the band's music didn't need to be understood that way. Although Adam and Chris continued to be credited as co-writers of the Fountains' songs, more obsessive fans, knowing that the two wrote independently of each other, scoured lyrics and chords for clues that might indicate whether a song was primarily written by Adam or by Chris. The results of this sleuthing occasionally generated strong debates among the Fountains' more devoted followers—but to some extent, the actual original author didn't really matter, because each writer indirectly influenced the other. Chris was the Fountains' only lead vocalist, so Adam had to write songs differently for the Fountains than he did for Ivy or any of his other projects, to fit Chris's vocal range and singing style. Likewise, Chris's lyrics often included the type of wordplay and sardonic perspectives that also showed up in Adam's writing. And neither of them could have made a song sound the way it did in their imaginations without Jody's and Brian's abilities to understand those ideas and bring them to life. So while either Adam or Chris might have written the first version of a song, the final product sounded the way it did because of what all four members of the band contributed to it.

Some writers cited the Fountains as one of many outstanding pop performers and songwriters—along with XTC, Aimee Mann, and the Rembrandts—that were being marginalized and made "culturally invisible" by the growing trend toward so-called alt-rock. Chris suggested that "'alternative' now means 'popular'" and that "every couple of years people start talking about a pop renaissance, but it never seems to happen." But one development making a pop renaissance more feasible was the World Wide Web, which was becoming more important as a way for power pop bands and independent labels to find their audiences, outside the traditional distribution and publicity channels of major labels. Power pop fans were using the web to share their enthusiasms, exchanging recommendations, newsletters, and updates on their favorite bands, and sharing tracks through sites such as Napster.

To promote *Utopia Parkway*, the Fountains toured for nearly nine months straight with only a few breaks. They started with an early April show at the Iron Horse in Northampton, headed to Europe for late April and May, and then trekked to US and European festivals over the summer. Adam's friend Steven Gold came along as a keyboard player, giving the band the ability to do fuller live versions of their songs. The shows drew audiences that Chris characterized as "teenage boys or girls who heard us on the radio, and then we skip up a number of years to these older pure pop fanatics—guys from New Jersey with big record collections who want to come up to us after the show and talk about the Shoes or the Raspberries." A reviewer of the band's June show in Philadelphia pointed out that the Fountains' audiences also often included "record label reps and local radio types who profess their love for the band, but don't actually give its records airplay."

As in previous years, there was the occasional disaster on tour. After a May show in Baltimore, the band got on the tour bus and headed for Boston—and left Brian behind. "We honestly didn't realize he wasn't on the bus until like fifteen minutes before the show," Adam recalled. "We thought he was in catering or something. But one of the guys at our label used to be a drummer, and he came up to us and was like, 'I know all your songs, dude, let me do it.' Mostly, he was good."

But as before, both Adam and Chris found it difficult to keep going with their songwriting on the road. "There have been times when I've written something just to force myself to do it," Adam admitted. "It's hard for me to write on tour," Chris told an interviewer in England, "because I'm so tired all the time. But I'm not worried about it. We wrote the first album in a week and recorded it in a week, and I'd rather wait to write everything." In late September the Fountains made their first trip to Australia—Gigolo Aunts guitarist Phil Hurley filled in for Jody, who was unable to go—and stopped in Japan again on the way back. The band's popularity in Japan was recognized by releases of several Japan-only singles from *Utopia Parkway* and by the video for "Troubled Times" being filmed while the band was playing there. The Fountains finished off the year with US dates in late November through mid-December, including a memorable show at New York's Fez Under Time Cafe. In addition to the now-expected medley of song snippets during "Radiation Vibe," that set included several full-length covers: Ron Sexsmith's "Nothing Good," Ricky Nelson's "Travelin' Man," and Paul Kelly and the Messengers' "Careless."

But Fountains of Wayne were now encountering even more difficulties with Atlantic. Despite the band's hard work, and the praise for *Utopia Parkway*, the relationship between the band and the label was fragmenting. "Denise" became a Top 10 single in Japan, but *Utopia Parkway* didn't produce a US hit single, despite four tries ("Denise," "Red Dragon Tattoo," "Troubled Times," and "The Valley of Malls"). Dave Walker of the *Arizona Republic*, in a lengthy article praising the band and *Utopia Parkway*, stated that "although earning priceless high-brow media exposure, the album couldn't find a home on radio among all the R&B divas, rapping rockers, and boy bands." He quoted Adam as saying, "We don't fit in with the Limp Bizkits and the Korns and Offspring, but we're not sort of soft enough to be an adult mainstream kind of thing either." Kurt Reil of New Jersey power pop band the Grip Weeds told journalist Robert Makin, "It's ironic that such radio-friendly music can't get on the radio." Makin also observed, "The increasingly consolidated music industry is more interested in creating media sensations such as the Backstreet Boys and Ricky Martin." It didn't help matters for the Fountains that some of their champions at Atlantic, such as Michael Krumper, had moved on to other jobs.

Chris said, "We've heard that we are the most played band on other bands' tour buses, and that is a lot better, in some ways, than having a hit single in a business where everything is a cartoon." But being well regarded by peers and critics, and having a fervent fan base, wasn't enough in an increasingly profit-oriented business. In December 1999, Atlantic dropped Fountains of Wayne from its roster. "To their credit," Adam said, "they didn't pull the plug on us in the middle of recording or shelve a record." Nonetheless, the year ended with the band label-less, impoverished, and discouraged.

6. GETTING TIRED OF THE TWISTS AND TURNS

A t the turn of the millennium, Fountains of Wayne faced an uncertain future. "I wasn't sure if I wanted to continue," Chris recalled. "At the end of four years of the hardest work I'd ever done in my life, more traveling and being away from my wife the whole time, I had nothing to show for it. I got back home and I had nothing. I was broke, I was demoralized, I was exhausted." Adam admitted that "we didn't know if there would be any interest in making another record." David Lindquist, a columnist at the *Indianapolis Star*, expressed similar concerns about the direction in which the popular music landscape was evolving: "Contemporary bands such as Guided by Voices and Fountains of Wayne— despite intensely melodic material—don't have a prayer in today's aggressive and angst-propelled rock climate." And Elton John, one of the band's most high-profile fans, was blunt about how poorly he felt Fountains of Wayne had been treated by the music industry. "*Utopia Parkway* was one of my favorite albums [of 1999], but the label did nothing to promote it."

Fountains of Wayne only played a few live dates in 2000, while the band members considered their options. In June, they played a festival at Naval Weapons Station Earle in Colts Neck, New Jersey, alongside John Eddie and Gary U.S. Bonds, as well as a circus and a professional wrestling show. The naval station opened to the public once a year for the event, with the concert stage placed on the baseball field, surrounded by "cannons and weapons on display," according to the high school student assigned by the local paper to review the gig. Brian was unable to participate and was replaced by "our good friend Allan [*sic*]" (Alan Bezozi from They Might Be Giants), as introduced by Chris. The festival was also memorable because, as Adam later recalled, "Apparently we were cursing, which no one seems to remember, and we weren't supposed to be drinking on the base, but there was all this alcohol in the trailer and we got into all kinds of trouble."

The following night, the band played a largely acoustic show at Maxwell's in Hoboken, which was notable for one of the rare live outings of the Pinwheel-era song "Half a Woman," and one of a very few performances of a number titled "Bowling Shoes." It was also the live debut of two other songs, "Hackensack" and "Mexican Wine," which would later become significant in the band's career.

But beyond those occasional gigs, and contributing a one-off song, "Too Cool for School," to the soundtrack of the film *Scary Movie*, the band members kept busy with their own activities. Adam and Chris continued writing songs that they hoped would be suitable for another Fountains album, while Chris played some solo shows, including appearing as a duo with his friend Philip Price of the Northampton-based band the Maggies. He also was part of the Gay Potatoes, a group of local friends that initially included Lloyd Cole, who had moved from New York to

Northampton. Cole had become friends with Chris and Adam after they met at the WXOU Radio Bar; he joined the Gay Potatoes on the understanding that it would be a covers band, but left as soon as the rest of the band members announced their intention to play original music. Primly referred to as the "Potatoes" by some of the local press, the band included several of Chris's original tunes in its sets, including "Cry One Tear" from the Pinwheel era. Jody was working on songs with NYC band The Astrojet, and Brian played sessions for several acts. Adam was working on the next Ivy album, *Long Distance*, writing several songs for the film *Josie and the Pussycats*, and co-writing and producing for other artists.

Josie and the Pussycats was a live-action film about an all-girl band, based on characters from the Archie comic books and the spin-off seventies TV cartoon series of the same name. The film itself was not a huge hit, but its soundtrack album was a success. Adam was just one of a long list of songwriters who contributed to the film's music, along with Jane Wiedlin of the Go-Go's, Kay Hanley of the Fountains' Boston friends Letters to Cleo, Jason Falkner, Babyface, and Adam Duritz. One song, "Come On," had ten credited co-writers, including Adam. In describing his work on the soundtrack to Tom Moon of the *Philadelphia Inquirer*, Adam provided some insights into what he perceived the music business now wanted in a song: "The thing you're limited to is the chord structure. Singles these days are not about chord changes, they're about grooves. Everything's loop-based. So the idea of writing a song where the pre-chorus has different chords, or the bridge goes to a different key, people don't think like that now."

In July 2001, Adam and Chris participated in a multi-act show at Northampton's Iron Horse, which must have been a very busy night for them: full sets by Ivy and the Gay Potatoes, with a four-song acoustic set of Fountains of Wayne tunes in between. Ivy's album *Long Distance* had just been released in the US, after being launched six months earlier in Japan. Like the Fountains, Ivy had a strong following there. The Fountains' set was "like a maxi-single of hits," said a reviewer, "which they were. Well, maybe not on Casey Kasem terms, but definitely for those souls in the world who constantly search out bands that write great pop songs."

In the fall, the entire world was shaken by the terrorist attacks of 9/11, which were especially devastating to everyone in and around New York City. Like many other nightly TV shows, Conan O'Brien's late-night talk show, which was based in New York, went off the air for a week after the attacks. O'Brien had previously featured Fountains of Wayne several times on his show, and when it started up again, he asked the band to perform on one of the first episodes after the return. The Fountains chose to play the Kinks' "Better Things," which Adam and Chris used to cover with their various college bands. "It was very hard to get a comedy show going under those circumstances," O'Brien reminisced, "and we were looking for people to help. Fountains of Wayne came on the program that first week we were back. It was such a special moment, and I couldn't imagine a better song for people to be listening to." On September 21, wearing red, white, and blue lapel ribbons to honor the dead and the first responders, the Fountains performed a powerful version of the song, conveying its timely sentiment of optimism in the face of sadness. A few months later, they recorded "Better Things" for *This Is*

Where I Belong, an album of covers of songs by Ray Davies and by the Kinks that was produced by O'Brien's music coordinator, Jim Pitt.

Another project that was offered to the Fountains in late 2001 was something that had been in the works for a while. A few years previously, VH1, a music video cable TV channel that was a mellower version of its corporate cousin MTV, had approached *Time* magazine columnist Joel Stein about creating an animated show for the channel. Stein's journalistic shtick was poking holes in self-absorbed celebrity culture, sometimes successfully and well deserved, sometimes less so. Stein proposed a show about a magazine writer named Joel Stein who interviewed celebrities on his VH1 talk show—the sort of meta-referential premise that made *It's Garry Shandling's Show* so influential on late eighties TV comedies. As Stein's show gradually came together and the pilot episode was being planned, its producers asked Fountains of Wayne to contribute songs to the pilot and to write the series' theme song—and to appear in the show as animated versions of themselves. The show's characters were designed by *New Yorker* cartoonist Robert Risko, who clad the cartoon Fountains in snazzy three-piece white suits.

The pilot for what was now titled *Hey Joel* was completed in early 2002. VH1 liked the pilot enough to commission thirteen episodes, and Fountains of Wayne were hired to provide two songs for each episode. Not only was that a considerable amount of music to write, perform, and produce, but the songs also had to reference the relevant characters and the key events of each episode's plotline. Stein later claimed that *Hey Joel* was the most expensive series that VH1 ever commissioned, and that the channel was only able to afford to produce the show because "the station hired Canadian animators and a Canadian supporting actor, which brought in Canadian government funding in what may be the most wasteful use of Canadian tax dollars since the country went bilingual."

As it turned out, the Fountains' musical interludes for *Hey Joel*, illustrated with very creative animation, were often the best parts of the episodes. Songs such as "Meet in the Middle," performed by the cartoon Fountains in a fantastical *Yellow Submarine*–style landscape, were as clever and well written as many of the tracks on the band's own albums. *Hey Joel* scored the occasional on-target jibe at pompous rock stars—the show's animation director said, "We were allowed to do some ludicrous things with the characters, as long as it was legal"—and got in some good jokes about VH1 being an afterthought in the Warner Communications hierarchy. The workplace antics of the cartoon Joel and his misfit gang of coworkers were also occasionally amusing. But the writing was generally uneven and sometimes didn't even make sense, especially when it singled out celebrities whose public personas were already evolving into self-parody.

After the thirteen *Hey Joel* episodes were completed, VH1 declined to commission another series, and sat on the finished episodes for more than a year. But because of the Canadian financing, the series had also been sold to Canadian cable TV, and all the *Hey Joel* episodes aired several times on the Bravo channel in Canada. While *Hey Joel* was something of a dud for its creators and for VH1, the Fountains' work on it paid well enough that they could cover the costs of recording another album themselves. They had also earned some additional income from another TV cartoon project, writing and performing the theme song for *Crank Yankers*, a Comedy Central series in which puppets voiced by celebrities made prank phone calls to unsuspecting customer service representatives.

Being able to afford to make their own album gave the Fountains the freedom of not having to rely on a record label for financial support, and the freedom to do what they wanted musically. Nonetheless, the process of recording a new album took a while to get going because, according to Adam, Chris needed more time to write. "I was definitely burned out," Chris admitted. "Chris wasn't writing a lot," Adam later recalled. "I don't know if it was the whole thing of being in between labels or more just the whole thing of putting all that time into it and feeling it tapering off. We started working on the third record, because it was the only way that I could get Chris to want to be a part of it. I was just like, 'Hey look, let's just go in and do like we have always done [since] we were eighteen. If we have a song we like, we'll just record it and eventually we'll see if we have an album.'" Jody described that time as feeling like "we didn't know where we were going. We didn't have a label, so we just kind of set up shop to see if we could come up with anything."

The band went to the Clubhouse, a studio in rural upstate New York, and laid down the backing tracks for four songs: "No Better Place," "Mexican Wine," "Bought for a Song," and "Stacy's Mom." "Once we had those four songs," Jody said, "we felt like we could get some interest from another record label and basically pay ourselves back."

They then hunkered down in Q Division studio in Somerville, near Boston, which was owned and operated by their longtime friend Mike Denneen. (The studio's name was a nod to the British Secret Service's technology development department in the James Bond films.) "We had been dropped by our label," Adam said, "but Mike worked with us for nearly two years on a new album anyway." The band took a break to play a live show in nearby Cambridge in March 2002, and debuted "Valley Winter Song," which had been recorded during the Q Division sessions.

Additional recording took place at Adam's Stratosphere Sound studio. "Between the two [studios]," Chris said, "since we weren't really paying for them, we could kind of afford to run up some debt, realizing eventually that it would come out somewhere." In the end, the Fountains completed nearly twenty new tracks. "We didn't sit down and map out some kind of concept or anything like that for the album," Adam later explained. "We just wrote what we wanted to write." "It's all over the map," Chris said, "and despite what the major labels think, it's a good thing." More importantly, though, a record company wouldn't have to wait for the Fountains to get their act together and do something; the band had an album ready to go. They just had to find a record company that had enough confidence to sign them.

7. GOT IT GOIN' ON

In late 2002, the Fountains made a deal with S-Curve Records, a subsidiary of Virgin Records' North American operations, to release their new album. Steve Yegelwel, one of their former champions at Atlantic, had taken an executive position at S-Curve, and the label had already had its first success with one of the ultimate one-hit wonder songs, the Baha Men's "Who Let the Dogs Out."

It was decided that rather than continuing to pitch Fountains of Wayne as an "alternative" act, the label would focus on promoting them as pop artists. This change in strategy was intended to achieve two outcomes: grow the band's audience beyond "college airplay and [being] critics' darlings," and get them a genuine hit. The Fountains weren't necessarily averse to the idea of having their music on the charts; Adam's and Chris's old friend Mike Viola said, in reflecting on the band's early days, "The thrill and the gamble of breaking the Top 40 was really appealing to them." However, the Fountains were not always comfortable with their music being categorized as pop, especially as power pop. "It's a double-edged sword," Adam said of the "power pop" moniker. "It implies a certain level of craftsmanship and a certain amount of intelligence. But it can suggest this unhealthy fixation with a certain kind of songwriting and record-making that's been done to death. We want people who aren't obsessive record collectors to be able to like our music." But ultimately they were willing to take a chance on being positioned as a pop band, in order to maximize their chances of having a hit single. They believed a hit would bring them more fans, including fans with broader musical tastes, in the long run. "We're trying to make a statement this time out," Chris told a reporter, "that we're so much more than what you've heard. If we're going to do well in America, we're going to do it on our terms."

Meanwhile, Adam had turned his attention to completing Ivy's next album, a collection of cover versions. *Guestroom* was released in September 2002, and once Adam had concluded his promotional responsibilities for that album, the Fountains embarked on a series of November club dates across the US, to try out some of the new album's songs for live audiences. Among the newly recorded numbers that debuted at these shows were "No Better Place," "Supercollider," and "Bright Future in Sales," which a Chicago reviewer described as a portrayal of "the even-when-you-win-you-lose irony of corporate work." That was a scenario that both Chris and Adam knew well, not only from their temp jobs but also from being part of the music business. "Most of your day is spent working, and it's no different being in a band," Adam explained to *Fast Company* magazine. "We're just business travelers, in a way, except instead of going to an office, we go to a club. It's identical [to corporate work] except that you occasionally have to write songs. In promotional mode, every day is a series of decisions, and you can easily fill up your day with checklist stuff."

Welcome Interstate Managers, as the third album was dubbed, was released in June 2003. The title suggested the cars-and-suburbia theme of its predecessor, but the cover was a bold statement that this album was heading somewhere else. The sleek Fountains of Wayne logo was superimposed on an old black-and-white photo, sourced from the archives of the New-York Historical Society, of tuxedoed businessmen solemnly seated around a circular table at a celebratory banquet. It certainly didn't look like the usual pop album cover, but this was not your usual pop album.

Like *Utopia Parkway*, the tracks on *Welcome Interstate Managers* boldly explored a range of musical styles. But this album went even further, with country ("Hung Up on You") and spacey psychedelia ("Supercollider") alongside pop music at its best. "Bright Future in Sales" was a dynamic depiction of a corporate climber whose ambition exceeded his competence, as he struggled with "*staring at the screen/ Pretending that I know what all these little flashing lights mean.*" The protagonist of "Little Red Light" sat frustrated on the Tappan Zee Bridge while his relationship fell apart— "*I'm still a mess and you still don't care*"—and no one left messages on his "*plastic Japanese cordless phone*" or his "*big black laptop.*" Some of the album's greatest moments, though, were in the quieter material: the genuinely touching "Hey Julie," with its depiction of a loving relationship offsetting the despair of a depressing workplace, and the comfortable familiarity of an early evening at home in "Yours and Mine." The diverse musical styles were tied together by a sense of confidence—not arrogance, but the sureness of a group playing as a unit and making the most of it. Singer-songwriter Robbie Fulks later observed, "Think of Adam's bass playing, Jody's guitar style, or Brian's drumming. On other records, in other groups, they might play differently and be hard to recognize. On Fountains of Wayne records, they're actually working in tandem so as not to make a big impression as stylists. They're curtailing themselves, limiting their spontaneous reflexes, and making a calculatedly unified group sound, which in turn clears more room for you to focus on what does express strong personality in their music: Chris's singing, and the songs."

As usual the songs were credited to Chris and Adam, but both acknowledged that while they had contributed an equal number of songs to *Utopia Parkway*, the majority of the songs on this album were written by Adam. "If it's a song about New Jersey or about teenagers," Chris said, "it's Adam's song." Jody later mentioned that "Hey Julie" was one of the few songs on *Welcome Interstate Managers* that still sounded relatively close to how it was originally presented to the full band. "'Let's try a 'Me & Julio' thing,' and we were like, 'OK, I guess . . .' We hadn't even picked it up in the rehearsal room. Fountains of Wayne's MO was to go to a preproduction studio in New York called Euphoria, and work out our songs, just so we were vaguely familiar with them. But they came in as campfire songs. Parts changed; solos were added." The scenes described in the lyrics of "Bought for a Song," according to Chris, were a "montage of things that happened to us on tour," including a memorable incident where Brian had to pull a drunken Jody out of the tour van amid a screaming crowd of fans who thought the van contained the Backstreet Boys.

"Valley Winter Song" was Chris's meditation on his experiences with seasonal affective disorder during the long, dreary New England winters. The lyrics name-checked the

Bay State, a dingy Northampton hotel bar described by one regular as "a major hang-out spot . . . where bands who were drawing attention all over the world could be playing in a space not unlike your living room." "Hackensack" was one of the standout tracks, with its touching portrayal of the pensive narrator stuck in New Jersey while the girl of his dreams became a star elsewhere. "Choosing Hackensack [as the setting] immediately helped focus the song," Adam explained. "You have this contrast between New Jersey and this imaginary Hollywood he's thinking of."

Welcome Interstate Managers was produced by Chris, Adam, and Mike Denneen. Denneen pointed out that one of the distinctive features of the album's sound was the use of keyboards; this was perhaps not too surprising because of Adam's piano skills and Denneen also being a keyboardist, but it wasn't a common production choice at the time. "We didn't say, 'Let's go for a big keyboard sound'; it happened organically," Denneen said a few years later. "I used to be the guy that threw them on because nobody had a keyboard player. Now you hear more and more of it."

Tom Kielty in the *Boston Globe* commented on *Welcome Interstate Managers'* "sunny power-pop ditties with subversive sentiments . . . while the band may have escaped a more mundane existence, they have never lost sympathy for those who haven't." That same contrast was noted by Sean Moeller in the *Muscatine Journal*, who said, "This album delves into sadness much as [*Fountains of Wayne*] leapt into glee like a child jumping into a pool of balls at a McDonald's Playland." Glenn Gamboa said in *Newsday* that "for the characters [in the songs] the limit is too painfully real, but Schlesinger and Collingwood almost always leave their characters an escape . . . it manages to keep the whole life lesson entertaining." In the *Honolulu Advertiser*, Derek Paiva praised the album for its "knowing character sketches and soliloquies for working stiffs, wrapped in a warm hoodie of woozy pop hooks, imaginative lyrics, and shimmering guitar hooks." The narratives in the songs, said Greg Kot of the *Chicago Tribune*, "are littered with details that will be familiar to anyone who has worked in or near a big city and yet somehow remains on the outside looking in when it comes to feeling a part of the excitement."

However, other critics were less impressed. Andrew Griffin in the *Town Talk* called the album "dark" and felt that the band "seemed a bit tired and worn out." John Kenyon of the *Cedar Rapids Gazette* felt that *Welcome Interstate Managers* was perhaps the band's best work, but "if anything, it's a bit long, and 16 songs is too much." Adam acknowledged in an interview that "there are all different tempos and volumes and melodies; I don't think any two songs sound the same."

The song that immediately stood out, though, to those who heard the album before its release was "Stacy's Mom." Adam somewhat shamefully admitted that it was inspired by an event in his early teens, when one of his friends told him that his grandmother was "hot." With its multilayered vocal harmonies, polished production, and unabashed sonic nods to the sound of the Cars, it was gloriously catchy ear candy. But despite "Stacy's Mom" being so appealing, there was some hesitation within the band about making it the first single from the album. With its lyrics describing an adolescent boy's sexual longing for what would later become known as a MILF, promoting "Stacy's Mom" ran the risk of Fountains of Wayne being categorized as the macho frat-boy guitar spankers that they definitely did not want to be. They might also be dismissed as purveyors of novelty songs—a particularly sensitive point for the band given the previous conflict over their cover of "…Baby One More Time."

Before the album was released, Chris had said, "If an A&R guy heard the album, he would search for the quirky song and that would be the single. I don't want the one-liner track to be the song that becomes the video." But that was exactly what happened. "Stacy's Mom" became *Welcome Interstate Managers'* first single. Reflecting the new strategy for promoting the band, the single was first released to rock radio, but was then additionally pushed to adult contemporary and Top 40 radio. It was also played to MTV president Judy McGrath. She expressed enough confidence in the song's visual potential for the Fountains' label to allocate a significant amount of money to create a music video.

At this point in MTV's history, the channel's programming had expanded to include its own shows, such as *The Real World, Total Request Live*, and *The Osbournes*, which were taking up an increasing amount of its airtime. With music videos nearing their second decade of ubiquity, videos were quickly becoming more elaborate and exaggerated in order to grab the attention of jaded viewers. One music industry executive looking back on this era described it as having "two conflicting curves: a rapidly climbing curve of expenses for a video, and a rapidly declining curve of the number of videos being exposed." In this "go big or go home" era, music videos had to be extravagant to have any chance at airplay.

The Fountains' label decided to go big with the video for "Stacy's Mom." It was directed by Chris Applebaum, who since making "Sink to the Bottom" with the Fountains had gone on to helm popular videos for artists such as Semisonic ("Closing Time"), Better Than Ezra ("Good"), and Hilary Duff ("So Yesterday"). Fountains of Wayne appeared in the video as black-and-white moving figures on magazine covers, a TV set, and wall posters, performing the song against backgrounds of vibrant purples and pinks. "Originally, we didn't want to be in the video at all," Adam later revealed, "but it worked out well and we weren't in it that much." And indeed, those clever settings for the band went almost unnoticed amid the high-end suburban fantasy played out in the rest of the video. Supermodel Rachel Hunter was chosen for the title role of the yummy mummy; apparently another supermodel, Paulina Porizkova, was also considered for the part—which would have been fitting, since at the time she was married to the Cars' Ric Ocasek—but Hunter was the band members' first suggestion, and she agreed to be in the video as soon as she was asked. "We couldn't believe it," Chris admitted.

The "Stacy's Mom" video was brilliantly constructed, full of visual nods to pop culture classics such as *Lolita* and *Fast Times at Ridgemont High*, and it celebrated the music video trope of sexy chicks while snickering at it. Regardless of whether viewers were laughing at the parody or drooling over Hunter in various skimpy outfits, "Stacy's Mom" quickly became one of MTV's biggest hits of summer 2003. The video was provocative enough that Fountains of Wayne—the store—got phone calls complaining about it; Brian Winter said, "I told people that called that we're not the band and the band isn't us."

Thanks to the, um, exposure from the video, "Stacy's Mom" shot up the charts. It reached #21 on the *Billboard* Hot 100 and made the Top 20 in Australia, Canada, Ireland,

Scotland, and the UK. "I think a lot of people within the industry were fans of the band when they were younger," Adam said, in trying to explain the single's success. "Maybe they played our first record on college radio, or were just starting out as journalists then, and now they've moved up the ladder, and they're in a position to help bands that they like." Sales were also helped by the arrival of legal (i.e., unlike Napster) online music-buying sites such as Rhapsody and iTunes, where "Stacy's Mom" was one of the most downloaded singles of the year—perhaps not surprising, since the song was not officially released as a CD single in the US. The only way for American fans to get their own copy of the song (legally) was to purchase the CD of the entire album. "Creatively speaking, we're big fans of the album as a medium," Adam told *USA Today*, addressing the reality that online sales tended to be purchases of individual tracks. "It's a little frustrating that people just cherry-pick songs, but we hope that if they like a song by us, they'll be curious and want to hear what else we've got."

"Stacy's Mom" pushed Fountains of Wayne from being what one of their fans, Matthew Caws of Nada Surf, described as "a slightly invisible band" into being a band with a hit song, and into experiencing all the baggage that came with that status. "There's nothing worse than having a big novelty hit," Chris reflected several years later. "People know you for one thing, and that's how they know you from then on. On the other hand, you can't really wish it undone because there's no saying how much attention that record would have gotten at all had people not heard that single." Adam's take on it was that "people all of a sudden know you for this one song. It just follows you around, and you have to play it over and over again. It comes to define you, but you have to find a way to stay fresh with it and enthusiastic about it. It's a weird thing." He regularly drew a parallel between Fountains of Wayne being known for "Stacy's Mom" and Randy Newman, one of his and Chris's songwriting heroes, being known for "Short People" rather than for his many other musical accomplishments.

Nonetheless, the single also seemed to tap into a large but largely overlooked group of music fans: those who were tired of ridiculously theatrical songs by ridiculously over-the-top musicians, and who wanted to see relatable people playing well-written songs about relatable topics. Craig Marks, the editor of *Blender* magazine, described the Fountains this way to the *New York Times*: "They are in their mid-thirties and don't look, sound or dress particularly cool, which makes them very cool in a way. They understand the middle-management dance of fear that so many people are doing in a downsizing era." Steve Yegelwel told the *Los Angeles Times*, "They never stopped being great. I would argue that they've only gotten better. My frustration in the past was that when you're on a very large record label, not every act is going to get a push at Top 40 or even a legitimate shot at Top 40 radio. I always thought that they deserved it."

"Stacy's Mom" also started popping up in unlikely places: an adaptation by a "Christian parody rock band" that recast it as "J.C.'s Mom"; as a sing-along spirit-raiser for sports teams and youth groups; and as a playlist staple at school dances—which might seem inappropriate given the mature subject matter, but the easy-to-sing chorus and classic pop arrangement appealed to kids. An eighth-grade boy told his local newspaper, "It has a nice beat. I don't like that he's talking about a girl's mom, but most people like it because the guy singing it has a nice voice." There were also fan-made re-creations of the video using the graphics and characters from *The Sims* video game, some of which actually aired on MTV2's series *Video Mods*. VH1 capitalized on the Fountains' sudden popularity by finally airing three *Hey Joel* episodes during a single week in June—the only time the show ever appeared on the channel. The Bravo channel in Canada continued rerunning all thirteen episodes of *Hey Joel* for the rest of the year and throughout 2004.

The success of "Stacy's Mom" put Fountains of Wayne back on the road for almost half of 2003. They hit the summer festival circuit and then returned to Japan for a few dates in the early fall. There were occasional detours to play benefit shows, such as the acoustic set that Adam and Chris performed in June at the Housing Works used bookstore in New York City, and an August concert in Northampton, where Chris and other local musicians raised funds for arts education in the region's schools; Chris and Philip Price took turns being Michael Stipe in front of a band for a set of R.E.M. covers.

At the Fountains' shows, "Stacy's Mom" caused varied reactions. The band tended to place the song early on in the set, usually following it with some of their older and more proven audience pleasers. But at more than one show, reviewers noticed groups of concertgoers leaving after the big hit single had been played. Those audience members missed most of what was usually a very strong live performance, but it must have been discouraging for the band.

In late summer, some fans' and industry insiders' eyebrows were raised when Fountains of Wayne were announced as the opening act for Matchbox Twenty on a US arena tour starting in mid-October and running through mid-December. The two bands had interestingly parallel histories, as both had signed to Atlantic Records around the same time, and their debut albums were released on the same day in 1995. Paul Doucette, Matchbox Twenty's drummer, recalled that when his band went to Atlantic to request more promotional support for that first album, "they were like, 'You know what, we're busy right now with Fountains of Wayne and we don't really care.'" But thanks to the single "3AM" becoming an unexpected hit, that first Matchbox Twenty album, *Yourself or Someone Like You*, sold nearly twelve million copies. The band was now going on tour to promote its third album, *More Than You Think You Are*.

Adam had an explanation for the Fountains' decision to accept a gig as Matchbox Twenty's opening act, even though they currently had their own hit single. "They're a massive band with a very open-minded audience. I think that a lot of people that listen to that band aren't necessarily exposed to a lot of new stuff—they're not necessarily seeking it out. And this is a way for them to hear us." Matchbox Twenty themselves were very glad to have the Fountains open for them; lead guitarist Kyle Cook enthused, "Everybody in the band is a fan, and why that first album didn't catch on is one of the biggest musical mysteries of the past ten years." And the Fountains certainly had fun on the tour. One arena manager mentioned that the dressing room requirements in the band's performance contract included "a pack of tube socks, one kitten, a Ken Griffey Jr. poster, and a mixtape of music that someone locally made, so they can listen to it while they're getting dressed." (The arena staff fulfilled the "kitten" request with a stuffed toy, since the contract didn't specify that it had to be a *real* kitten.)

The Fountains also pranked Matchbox Twenty by asking a favor of satirist Robert Smigel, whom Adam knew from writing music for Smigel's TV segments on *Saturday Night Live*. The band got Smigel to make a video of his caustic puppet Triumph the Insult Comic Dog being rude about Matchbox Twenty, and played it on the onstage video screens during one of the headliners' sets. Singer Rob Thomas said one of his favorite memories from that tour was "Triumph on the screen at the back mocking us."

"I frankly didn't know much of [Matchbox Twenty's] music before the tour," Chris said, "but by the end, you realize why that band has such popular appeal. Those songs are so hummable." However, it was debatable whether it was wise for a band three albums into its career *and* with a major hit single (and video) to tour as an opening act. That spot on concert bills was traditionally the place for new or relatively unknown bands—and as the Fountains had found out at the start of their touring career, opening acts generally got smaller and less attentive crowds than the headliners. Reviews of the Fountains' performances on the Matchbox Twenty tour were appreciative, although descriptions such as "fast-rising" and "future headliners" must have stung at least a little for a band that already had extensive touring and recording experience.

But the Fountains' management had bigger plans for the band, and the Matchbox Twenty booking apparently was part of those plans. Q Prime co-owner Cliff Burstein told the *New York Times*, "If someone can be the leader in their category, we have an interest in that. We are not looking for them to be a cult band. We want them to be as big and popular as they can be. Right now they have a popular song and a popular video." He also semi-jokingly told *Blender* magazine, whose correspondent was playing "manager for a day" with the Fountains, "You have to constantly remind them that this is no slam-dunk. They have to work their asses off. Remind them of their history: We've had disappointing sales; we were dropped by our label. When they turn around and ask you 'Why the fuck are we in Pittsburgh again?' your job is to remind them just how hard it has been in the past."

The banner year of 2003 ended with several high-profile recognitions for the band. *Welcome Interstate Manager* was on numerous end-of-year "Best Albums" lists, including those in magazines such as *MOJO, The Word, Rolling Stone, Q,* and *Blender.* The Fountains of Wayne store honored the band with its own diorama in the 2003 Christmas Extravaganza; the store's newspaper ads proclaimed, "Fountains of Wayne (The Store) Salutes Fountains of Wayne (The Band)." And the Fountains were included in the "sexy singers" section of *People* magazine's annual "Sexiest Man Alive" issue. But one honor was simultaneously welcome and baffling. When the nominations for the 46th Annual Grammy Awards were announced in December, Fountains of Wayne received two nods: one in the category of Best Pop Performance by a Duo or Group with Vocal, for "Stacy's Mom" (another nominee in the same category was their tour mates Matchbox Twenty, for "Unwell"), and one in the Best New Artist category.

The Best New Artist category at the Grammys was already controversial. In past years it had regularly included nominations for artists that were anything but new. Some music writers had taken to calling the Best New Artist Grammy the Shelby Lynne Memorial Award, after Lynne was nominated, and won, in 2001 although she had already released six albums. The award had also been dubbed the Career Kiss of Death Award, since more than a few past winners never had another hit after getting the award. It was also the only Grammy category that had ever had an award revoked; 1990 winners Milli Vanilli had their Grammy taken away after it was revealed that they did not actually sing on "their" record.

Even with those past absurdities, there was an outcry at Fountains of Wayne being considered "new" after releasing three albums within seven years. Steve Morse of the *Boston Globe* called the nomination "the most bizarre choice in any of the Grammy categories." Andrew McGinn of the *Springfield News-Sun* sarcastically commented, "I guess that was a different Fountains of Wayne that I reviewed for my college paper, oh, six years ago." The rather half-hearted explanation from the Recording Academy was that nominations for Best New Artist were intended to recognize "a new artist who releases, during the eligibility period, the first recording which establishes the public identity of that artist." The criteria sounded reasonable, albeit somewhat subjective—how could anyone meaningfully measure whether a "public identity" had been successfully "established"?—but they also didn't seem to apply to any of that year's Best New Artist nominees. In addition to the Fountains, the category included 50 Cent, who had released an EP and several hit mixtapes; Evanescence, who had only just released their first full album; Sean Paul, who had released two albums; and Heather Headley, who had starred in two Broadway shows and won a Tony Award for Best Actress in a Musical. "It's nice to feel part of what's going on, instead of feeling ignored," Adam diplomatically observed. "But looking at [the nomination] as some sort of validation, well, that can be troubling."

8. A STRANGE AND FOREIGN PLACE

Although it was exciting for Fountains of Wayne to finally have a hit single, the band was realistic about what the success of "Stacy's Mom" might mean for their careers in the long run. "We really didn't know if anyone would notice when we put this record out," Adam told the *Los Angeles Times*. "If we were 21 years old, we might be deluded into thinking it would always be like this. But we've been through so much already that we see it for what it is." But one of the many unexpected consequences of having a hit single is the pressure to have another hit. "Our manager has been saying to us," Adam revealed, "we've got to move faster this time around and not squander the momentum that 'Stacy's Mom' has created."

"Mexican Wine" was selected as the second single from *Welcome Interstate Managers*. It was an unconventional song that declared itself as such from the very first line—"*He was killed in a cellular phone explosion*"—but it had a catchy chorus, and an energetic arrangement punctuated by Jody's searing guitar chords. Since the video for "Stacy's Mom" had pushed that song onto the charts, the feeling was that the video for "Mexican Wine" had to be equally flashy to have the same impact. Chris Applebaum was hired as director, and the video was filmed in December 2003.

If the "Stacy's Mom" video went big, the "Mexican Wine" video went *really* big. This time, the band, clad in designer suits, played on the prow of a superyacht plowing through a tropical sea. The performance shots were intercut with scenes of the band members strolling on a beach and, somewhat uncomfortably, lip-syncing the song below deck while lingerie-clad women had a pillow fight in the background, and a troupe of bikini-wearing dancers wiggled their butts on the top deck. "The video shoot was crazy," Chris said. "We were out in LA on a yacht off Malibu. Girls in bikinis. Helicopter shots of the beach. Some mariachi band." The video seemed to be intended as a satire of rock star video excess, and it had some clever visual shout-outs to classic music videos like Duran Duran's "Rio." But the whole thing felt a little too much like an unsuccessful imitation of that sort of video, rather than a parody. A lavish seagoing yacht also seemed an odd setting for a band whose regular-person relatability was part of its appeal.

As it turned out, awkwardness wasn't the only problem with the "Mexican Wine" video. The setting for the opening and closing verses of the song was a cheesy TV talent show called *Star Seekers*. This was clearly intended as a jibe at the hugely popular *American Idol*; the actual host of *Idol*, Ryan Seacrest, was booked to play the talent show host, but he had to drop out because of a scheduling conflict and was replaced by Drew Carey. The contestants on *Star Seekers* were two identical blond tween girls with a guitar and a keyboard, pretending to play the song. In the opening scene, when they sang "I think I'll have another glass of Mexican wine," one of them mimed opening a bottle, pouring something into a glass, and chugging it. The closing scene, according to a newspaper columnist who saw the full version of the original video, was one girl standing behind a kitchen counter, singing the final verse while lifting a saucepan lid to reveal her sister's head simmering in a pot of beans (a homage to Wall of Voodoo's video for "Mexican Radio").

No one thought anything of this at the time—and why would they? MTV was airing far more outrageous content every single day. But the "Mexican Wine" video was delivered to MTV in February 2004, right after "Nipplegate"—the incident at the 2004 Super Bowl halftime show, when Justin Timberlake tore off part of Janet Jackson's top and exposed her breast to millions of TV viewers. The US Federal Communications Commission used this alleged "wardrobe malfunction" as an excuse to crack down on perceived indecency in broadcasting, and TV networks suddenly became hyper-sensitive to airing anything that might not be considered family friendly. Someone at MTV decided that it was too risky to show a tween girl pretending to have an alcoholic drink and then apparently becoming a cannibal, and the "Mexican Wine" video was shelved. An edited version was later briefly broadcast on the channel, including the mimed drinking, but replacing the bean-pot scene with Carey thanking the girls as the glittery stage curtains closed behind them. The lack of visibility for the "Mexican Wine" video hurt the single's momentum, and "Mexican Wine" failed to chart. "Hey Julie" was later released as a third single, but that also missed the charts.

The Grammy Awards ceremony was held in February 2004. Chris, Adam, Jody, and Brian dutifully walked the red carpet at LA's Staples Center and got some media flak from fashionistas for their appearance. "Great song," one sniped, "but get a collective haircut. None of you looks like Ashton Kutcher." The ceremony itself turned out to be something of a bore. "The only time I thought something was going to happen was when the people told us to stay in our seats," Chris grumbled. "They were like, 'Don't get up. You can't leave.' Of course it turned out that was just for camera angles." The Fountains departed the festivities empty-handed, losing to Evanescence for Best New Artist (which Adam had predicted) and to No Doubt's "Underneath It All" for Best Pop Performance by a Duo or Group with Vocals.

The Grammy ceremony was a brief respite during a very busy year. Fountains of Wayne were on the road almost continuously from the end of January until the end of August. That touring schedule obviously gave them limited time to develop new songs or to record. And with a Top 30 single, the promotional duties for the band became even more intense. "The whirlwind carrying the band," observed Florida reporter Sean Piccoli, "[is] a business tornado of chart action, television appearances, and interviews by cellphones from somewhere on the road." Adam told Piccoli that he figured it was better to be sought after and overscheduled for now: "I won't complain. Maybe Chris will. But I won't."

Chris didn't exactly complain, but he also didn't hide the realities of the attention generated by a hit single. When a high school reporter asked him for advice on entering the music industry, he matter-of-factly told her, "We have to work really, really hard at this. You have to realize that we work all day, every day. We don't have weekends. Pursue music only if it's the one thing you are really good at."

In March, Fountains of Wayne returned to the UK, where, despite that being one of the strongest markets for their album and single releases, they had not played live since 1999. The *Daily Telegraph* reviewer who caught their show at the Astoria in London reported that "some of the crowd even engaged in a little light moshing" and that the show "wasn't especially profound, but it was affecting, it was melodic, and it was fun." During the UK jaunt, "Stacy's Mom" rose to #11 in the UK singles charts, which qualified the Fountains to appear on the BBC's long-running *Top of the Pops* TV show. They performed the song on the March 19 broadcast, and judging by their giddy grins, it was a dream come true for the self-declared Anglophiles.

Despite the band riding high with Grammy nominations and a hit single, some of their live bookings were unusual ones. In January, the Fountains opened for Cheap Trick at an Arizona concert that was part of the entertainment during a golf tournament. Chris pointed out that they actually didn't mind doing that show, because he was a golfer—"I'm not very good, but I love watching and playing"—and because the Fountains were huge Cheap Trick fans. In April, the band played a festival in California that also featured Jessica Simpson, Hilary Duff, Maroon 5, the Black Eyed Peas, and Nick Cannon. "It was totally geared at young kids, and we went on last because they assumed the kids would be gone by then," Adam said later. "But nobody left. We ended up in front of 30,000 screaming kids who assumed that because we were on last, we were the big stars, and we were out there with two acoustic guitars. It was pretty surreal."

It wasn't really the band's fault when a May gig in Boston fell on the same night as the TV broadcast of the last-ever episode of *Friends* on TV—although to their credit, the venue was almost three-quarters full despite the show being up against that pop-culture milestone. But later that month they played a Memorial Day beach festival in Delaware where, rather than being scheduled during the prime-time weekend evening slots, they performed an hour-long set at 10 p.m. Friday night "to a sparse crowd in a banquet hall." Nonetheless, Adam said that the band usually enjoyed playing summer festivals. "You get to pop into a few places, hang out with a lot of different bands, and play for a diverse crowd." In June, along with John Mayer, the Darkness, and Velvet Revolver, the Fountains were one of the musical attractions at "Fantasy Island," a two-day extravaganza staged by *Maxim, Blender,* and *Stuff* magazines in a specially constructed venue on the Atlantic City shore. The ads for the event promised attendees that they would "rub shoulders with scorching hot celebrities [and] hang out in a hot tub full of *Maxim* girls"—although a journalist that attended the event reported that the girls were local part-time models hired for the weekend, the few D-list celebrities that showed up stayed inside the VIP tent, and the promised camel rides never materialized.

Meanwhile, Adam had taken on yet another significant commitment, in addition to his work with Fountains of Wayne and with Ivy. "He was incredibly ambitious," Dominique Durand said of Adam's continual juggling of multiple projects. "He was driven to success. But he had a fear of boredom. He was scared by it. I think he had to fill up his time to be involved with many things, because to him boredom was intolerable." In March, Adam signed on to co-write the music for *Cry-Baby*, a stage musical based on the 1990 John Waters film of the same name. In 2002 the musical *Hairspray*, based on another Waters film, was a major Broadway hit. *Cry-Baby*'s producers had already hired the two playwrights that adapted the *Hairspray* film for the stage, but they wanted new talent to create the music for the new show. Adam and his collaborator David Javerbaum, a writer for TV's *The Daily Show*, wrote and submitted two song demos to the musical's production team. Waters said that the song titled "Baby, Can I Kiss You with My Tongue?" was "the one that won me over. They're irreverent without being mean; they just seem to get it." The producers planned to bring *Cry-Baby* to Broadway in the spring of 2005.

But while Adam took on this new assignment, the pressure was growing on Fountains of Wayne to make a new album and capitalize on their current success—and have another hit single. The reality was, though, that as in previous years, the band could not tour and create a new album at the same time. It was also unclear whether "Stacy's Mom" had expanded the band's audience as much as had been anticipated. The commercial failure of the other two singles from *Welcome Interstate Managers* suggested that "Stacy's Mom" had not generated significantly more interest in the Fountains' music. And as Adam suggested a few years later, the band's long-term fans might not have been that interested in "Stacy's Mom" either. "I think the audiences, if they're going to actually bother to come and see an entire show of us, it's because they like more than just that one song," he said. "In fact, they probably don't even really want to hear that song."

In June, *Billboard* reported that the next Fountains of Wayne album would be a compilation of unreleased tracks, B-sides, and bonus tracks from non-US releases. It was a somewhat surprising strategy, since compilation albums like this were usually released by acts to finish up their careers, or to complete their contractual obligations. It was questionable whether fans who only knew the Fountains from "Stacy's Mom" would be interested in an album of rare tracks by a band that was relatively new to them. By now the Fountains had a core audience that hopefully would buy pretty much anything the band released, but there was also the very real possibility that many of those fans might already have acquired these tracks from buying the original singles and releases, from bootlegs, or through tape or file trading.

Regardless of whatever the Fountains decided to do next, Rachel Hunter wasted no time in making the most of the celebrity she had acquired from starring in the "Stacy's Mom" video. She posed for a pictorial in *Playboy* magazine (cover headline: "Stacy's Mom Is Naked"), signed up as an endorser for several beauty products, and participated in a reality show based on the classic TV series *Gilligan's Island*. The Fountains, however, slowed things down a bit. In August, they made a brief foray to the UK for two festival shows and a club gig. The club show was especially memorable because Glenn Tilbrook of Squeeze—one of their favorite bands—opened the show and then joined them for an encore of "Red Dragon Tattoo" and Squeeze's "Is That Love."

After returning home, the band stepped off the road to focus on writing songs for the next studio album, and to give Adam time to work on his other projects. A few individual tracks kept them visible, such as the acoustic version of "Everything's Ruined" that appeared on the *Future Soundtrack for America* benefit album, and the football-in-slow-motion epic "All Kinds of Time" being licensed by the National Football League to use in its promotional films and commercials. But as planning began for the next studio album, it was becoming more apparent that Chris was starting to struggle with alcohol abuse.

9. LOOKING FOR A NEW ROUTINE

The Fountains kept a low profile for the early part of 2005, with Chris and Adam working separately on songs for the next studio album. Adam was also working with Ivy on finishing that band's new album, *In the Clear*; he played some live dates with the band to promote it when it was released in March. "People think that Adam started in Fountains of Wayne and began Ivy as a side project," Dominique Durand told an interviewer. "But Fountains of Wayne was the side project. It was the band that happened to blow up commercially, but Ivy is still the original." Brian took advantage of the downtime to play shows in LA as part of Brotherhood of Lost Dogs, a band led by Eve 6 vocalist Max Collins.

A previously unheard Fountains track, "Tell Me What You Already Did," was included on the soundtrack for the animated film *Robots*, released in March. The band also made an appearance that month in an episode of the NBC-TV series *American Dreams*. The series followed the lives of the fictional Pryor family in the sixties and regularly included cameos by contemporary artists in the roles of musical acts from that era. The episode gave the Fountains the opportunity to perform as one of their all-time favorite bands, the Hollies, playing "Bus Stop" on *American Bandstand*. While the Fountains' performance was intercut with shots of characters talking in the studio audience, what was shown and heard indicated a very convincing cover of one of the Hollies' best songs, with Chris in a shaggy wig doing a credible impersonation of Hollies lead singer Allan Clarke.

"Stacy's Mom" also made a reappearance that month, as the soundtrack to a Dr Pepper TV commercial that parodied the song's now-famous video. A suburban cardigan-wearing mom greeted a group of drooling middle-school boys and opened her minivan's door to reveal . . . a cooler full of icy bottles of the drink. "I don't think we have a philosophical objection to having our songs used in commercials," Adam said, "but it has to be something that we can live with. In that case, what I liked about what they were doing was parodying our video." Chris added, "We got offered a gig to play for the corporation that makes Marlboro cigarettes, and that was kind of a no-brainer to say no. But I think Dr Pepper is kind of harmless."

That spring, Robbie Fulks released a single titled "Fountains of Wayne Hotline." The inspiration for the song, he said, came from a game that he and his bandmates used to play during long van rides, imagining how Adam's and Chris's songwriting expertise might work at a crisis center for aspiring songwriters. "In our game," he explained, "one of us would place an emergency call for counseling, and a member of a large bureaucratic labyrinth, usually harried and gruff, would offer a solution based on time-honored Fountains of Wayne techniques." Some angry Fountains fans interpreted the song as an insult to the band, by implying that its music was formulaic, but Fulks said that the song was intended as a tribute to "the band's super-competency and amazing consistency." He pointed out that it wasn't "nastily satirical toward the band. The satire, such as it is, is shallow; I revere their work." After the single came out, the Fountains invited Fulks to one of their shows so that they could meet in person, and Adam complimented him on the song.

The band went out on tour again in June, just as *Out-of-State Plates* was released, and used the opportunity to try out some new songs. "Strapped for Cash" and "Yolanda Hayes" were among the new numbers that occasionally popped up in that summer's set lists. Among those shows was a series of performances in various US cities to entertain runners in the 5K and 10K Run Hit Wonder road races, a series of recreational fun runs sponsored by Nike. The Fountains also participated in a fundraising concert staged at Fenway Park by Boston Red Sox manager Theo Epstein, with the proceeds going to Epstein's delightfully named charitable foundation for disadvantaged kids, the Foundation to Be Named Later.

"Maureen" was released as a single from *Out-of-State Plates*, and the album itself was released on Virgin Records, which originally distributed S-Curve's releases but had now taken over the label. As a compilation album, *Out-of-State Plates* was definitely of a higher quality than similar releases by other artists. It was cleverly sequenced, with audio clips from radio station coverage of the band opening each of the two CDs. The extensive, and often hilariously self-deprecating, liner notes by Adam and Chris gave context to both the new and the old material, along with providing some insights into the songs' histories. While some acts didn't put a lot of attention or effort into non-album tracks, the B-sides and bonus tracks on *Out-of-State Plates* showed that, if anything, the Fountains had more good material than they knew what to do with. Despite having originally been relegated to the status of add-ons to singles, tracks such as the powerful "You're Just Never Satisfied" ("*God only knows why I try to please you*"), the wry character study "Comedienne" ("*She knows there are gonna be times/When no one goes for her funniest lines*") and the energetic "Small Favors" were strong enough to stand on their own. Among these sat other gems, in addition to "Maureen." There were new recordings of "Half a Woman," "I Know You Well," and "Imperia" from the Pinwheel era; "The Girl I Can't Forget" (a reworking of "Bowling Shoes"); and the official release of the "...Baby One More Time" cover.

The new "Half a Woman" on *Out-of-State Plates* was recorded during breaks in the *Utopia Parkway* sessions. Adam told the Montclair newspaper that "Half a Woman" was his first attempt as a songwriter to emulate how Chris used his own life events and memories as the starting point for a song. In middle school, Adam saw the magician Great Scott perform at a friend's birthday party, and that became the inspiration for the sardonic tale of a hapless magician and his rebellious assistant. The newspaper managed to find Great Scott—which actually wasn't too hard, because Scott Drucker, a.k.a. Great Scott, was working as an account executive at another newspaper in the region and still moonlighting as a magician. Drucker had no idea about the song until an audience member at one of his shows told him about it. "The thing that I'll most enjoy is that even when I'm not around," he said, "my family can take that CD and play it and think about me. In a way, it's like having a minidocumentary made about my life."

Critical opinions on *Out-of-State Plates* were mixed. A high school student assigned by the *Pittsburgh Post-Gazette* to review the album felt that "most of the material isn't of the same quality as their previous albums, although some of it comes close." Several reviewers commented that as much as they enjoyed the Fountains' music, they felt that thirty tracks of it was a lot to wade through. "The album may not hold together thematically," Chris said, "but I still really like it."

In fall 2005, Gerry Beckley of the band America—best known for the seventies hits "A Horse with No Name" and "Sister Golden Hair"—revealed that Adam and James Iha were working with them on a new album. Adam and Mike Denneen were also involved in making *Greetings from Imrie House* by the Click Five, a power pop band with a New Wave fashion sensibility that was getting a big push from its label, Lava Records; Adam wrote "Just the Girl," which became a US Top 20 hit for the group. And by now Fountains of Wayne had been around long enough that one of their songs was anthologized in a decade-spanning retroactive compilation. "Radiation Vibe" was included in Rhino Records' *Whatever*, a "nineties pop and culture" box set that *Pitchfork* sneered was "seven discs and over a hundred dollars' worth of random nostalgia."

In October, the Fountains visited Chicago to record an episode of the PBS in-concert series *Soundstage*. Then toward the end of the year, all four band members went to a studio in Woodstock in upstate New York for a week, and jammed on a couple of song possibilities for the next album. Adam and Chris wanted to see if this approach would generate different perspectives than their usual method of each of them working on songs by themselves. "We tried something different," Adam revealed. "Chris and I wanted Jody and Brian to be more involved earlier on. It was fun." He also noted that the jams had resulted in "tons and tons of ideas [that] we didn't even try to make into songs on the spot. Now we've got to go back and make them into something. There are some other songs that are fully written that just haven't made it onto an album yet." But Chris was still mindful of letting songs happen as they needed to happen. "Some songs might take a little longer, but I don't think of songwriting in terms of ease or difficulty," he told *American Songwriter* magazine. "There will be a thing where I'll have a song where I know what it's about and it's missing a few lines. I just have to be patient until I have those lines, but I don't think of it as hard. But forcing a song can make it feel terribly wrong."

In December, the Fountains were honored once again in the Fountains of Wayne store's 2005 Christmas Spectacular. Their diorama was placed amid depictions of Santa filling in for chef Emeril Lagasse on the Food Network, Santa enjoying the attractions at the Jersey Shore, and Santa in a jungle as a contestant on the hit TV show *Survivor*. The band closed out the year with a New Year's Eve show at Navy Pier in Chicago, and took a few weeks off—except for Adam, who started his 2006 with an Ivy gig in New York City. He described to a curious reporter the process of balancing commitments to both bands: "Usually one band will be in a touring cycle, and the other will be writing material for a new record. As one thing winds down, the other picks up."

The Fountains played in January at the US Snowboarding Championships in New Jersey—a relatively high-profile gig, at least in the sports community, since the results of the event would determine the US snowboarding team for the upcoming Winter Olympics. The day of the concert, the winds on the slopes were so strong that the competitive events were postponed, but the show went on nonetheless. At the end of that month, after playing an acoustic gig as part of the American Songbook series at Lincoln Center in New York City, the Fountains headed to Japan. But by then Chris was struggling even more.

"It was depression and alcoholism and lack of sleep, and kind of running myself into the ground," he said a few years later. He had always been a restless sleeper, in addition to his problems with seasonal affective disorder during wintertime. Recently, he had started having "acid-trippy visions" of "my ex-girlfriend pulling poppies out of her head, poppies that weren't even there." After the band's arrival in Japan, Chris suddenly went into what he later described as a "total breakdown." Unable to sleep for four days straight, he was given anti-anxiety medication and put on a flight back to the US. He returned to his home to rest and recover, but he was still sleeping erratically. Then he started to see "shadow people": objects in his house that, fleetingly glimpsed, looked like humans to him.

Chris checked into the local hospital and stayed there for two weeks while his condition was stabilized. After he was released, though, the process of recovery was slow and gradual. During that time, he said several years later, "I was not doing well in a lot of different ways." His challenges meant that Adam had to take the creative lead on the next Fountains album, which the band was aiming to release at the end of 2006. The band was recording at Stratosphere Studios, which gave them some flexibility in their recording schedule and also allowed them to be with their families and friends. "Rather than blocking off a couple of months to make the album, we do it in little spurts," Adam told *Billboard*, "and work on a couple of songs at a time. That way it maybe doesn't seem quite so daunting." Jody later reflected on the same sporadic process. "Because we were in the game, we sort of played the game every three or four years, but I don't think anyone would accuse us of being the most prolific or the most ambitious band. We just sort of did it when we felt like it. But when we worked, we worked really hard."

In May 2006, the America album was officially announced for release in the fall—the band's first album of original material since 1997. Adam said that working with Bunnell and Gerry Beckley had been "a blast. They write timeless songs, and they are phenomenal singers and musicians." In between those sessions and the sessions for the Fountains album, Adam was also writing songs for the soundtrack of *Music and Lyrics*, a rom-com film starring Hugh Grant and Drew Barrymore. Adam got to know the film's writer and director, Marc Lawrence, when Lawrence used "Hat and Feet" in his 2002 film *Two Weeks Notice*. Adam received a "Music by" credit on *Music and Lyrics*, although he ended up writing only three of the film's songs—but he was involved in another important aspect of the film's creation. Grant was playing a former pop star trying to maintain a rapidly fading musical career, but, Adam said, Grant "had never listened to any pop music in his life and didn't know what it's supposed to sound like." That led to Adam, along with Martin Fry from eighties pop band ABC, coaching Grant—who was also not a trained vocalist—to convincingly perform the songs that Grant's character sang in the film. "One of the more surreal days I've ever had in the recording studio was Martin Fry teaching Hugh Grant his old dance moves,"

Adam recalled. "Showing him how to do the hair-flip and the point, and all these sort of trademark moves of his."

During the summer of 2006, the band played a few festival dates, including an event at the Appel Farm Arts and Music Center in New Jersey, where Adam had attended summer music camp as a teen. The performance that the band had recorded for *Soundstage* aired on PBS in July. Throughout the summer and fall, the recording sessions for the Fountains album continued whenever Adam was available, and whenever Chris was able to participate. "I was drunk a lot of the time," Chris said, "and I didn't contribute a whole lot. I only wrote three songs for the album." It was now also rare for either Chris or Adam to make demos of their songs; instead, they would each bring music and lyrics to rehearsals and collaboratively develop each song with the other band members. "Most of the time we just prefer being in the same room and having a rough idea of what we're going for," Chris explained, "and then just let the band come up with the arrangement. We worked that way almost exclusively for this record." Jody later noted that Chris's limited availability led to another change in the Fountains' sound. "[Because of] the lack of Chris being there, I had to fill in a lot of holes. So [this album] has got the most guitar."

Traffic and Weather was finally released in April 2007. The cover art, a collage of colorful Op Art–style graphic images, indicated that this album was full of surprises. But, perhaps unintentionally, it also signaled that this album was not as thematically coherent as Fountains of Wayne's previous studio albums. That was a potential problem, especially with increased attention to *Traffic and Weather* as the first album of all-new material after the album that included "Stacy's Mom." Chris's perspective was that "everybody knew that

["Stacy's Mom"] was a fluke [and] the song wasn't really as much of a hit as the video was." But the band's record label didn't completely share that opinion. Amani Duncan, the senior VP of marketing at Capitol Records (the Virgin label's distributor), told *Billboard* that the Fountains "superseded their core [audience] with that record [*Welcome Interstate Managers*], and you can't assume that audience will still be there. The consumer is a very fickle person. There are no guarantees." The marketing strategy for the new album, she said, was to "superserve the band's fan base but not necessarily give up the 'Stacy's Mom' converts." To draw in both audiences, a snippet of "Stacy's Mom" was played at the very beginning of TV ads for *Traffic and Weather*, as "a way to hook fans' attention for the new music."

Traffic and Weather had its moments, but overall it seemed to lack the verve and confidence of the band's earlier work. The playing was outstanding—Jody stated, "[It was] probably my best solo ever in 'This Better Be Good,' the best thing I ever contributed to those records. Adam and I came out there high-fiving after that one." There were also clever touches, like contrasting the voices of Chris and guest vocalist Melissa Auf der Maur on "Someone to Love" to underscore the lyrics of two lonely urban careerists. Many of the songs had solid premises, such as the "totally busted" cheater of "This Better Be Good" and the conniving shyster of "Strapped for Cash" with his claims of "*Give me a minute/You know you'll get it back.*" But once characters were introduced, the lyrical portrayals lacked the nuance and depth that had made the Fountains' music so captivating in the past. Some of the songs, like "Revolving Dora" and "New Routine," didn't really seem to go anywhere. And some songs fell far below the Fountains' usual standards. The gentle stoner anthem "Planet of Weed," Adam admitted, was pretty much made up in the studio—which was even more obvious from the chatter and random noises in the background of the track.

By now the Fountains' music was respected for its ability to accurately, and sympathetically, evoke the experience of ordinary jobs and day-to-day urban life. *Time* magazine characterized them as the band "who are to accountants what Bruce Springsteen is to refinery workers." Most reviewers of *Traffic and Weather* were familiar with the Fountains' past work, and most of them agreed that the band deserved its reputation for quality songwriting and musicianship. However, the reviews gave the impression that while writers were favorably disposed toward the Fountains' music and wanted to be positive about *Traffic and Weather*, they couldn't quite bring themselves to be as enthusiastic as they had been in the past. "The everydayness of the songs makes them relatable," said Eric Danton in the *Hartford Courant*, "but the album started to feel routine by the end." "They pile on the eighties synthesizers a bit too thick here, and there are tiny signs of being off their game," said David Bauder of the Associated Press. Brian McCollum of the *Detroit Free Press* highlighted "an overindulgence in lyrical wit" and called the album "often too self-consciously clever for its own good." Adam attributed some of the negative comments to "[being] an underdog band for a while and now being kind of an overdog band, so we had it coming."

In April, the Fountains went on tour to promote the album. A reviewer at one of the early shows noted that "they are a little older and less spontaneous," and also observed that only about half the songs from *Traffic and Weather* were included in the set. But other critics were more complimentary, praising the "irresistible melodies and a buoyant atmosphere," and the "enthusiastic, charged performances." The Fountains appeared for the first time at the Coachella Festival, playing in the California desert on an April day when temperatures in the region hit record highs. They made a trip to the UK in May and played throughout the US for most of that summer and fall, mostly as headliners, sometimes as the opening act for their friends Squeeze. They also returned to Japan twice, in July and in October. "For some reason we do better there than anywhere else," Adam explained.

But despite all the band's hard work and commitment, its record sales were not increasing. During the week that *Traffic and Weather* was released, the *Los Angeles Times* presented a comparison of previous album sales figures for three acts with new albums: Fountains of Wayne, Hilary Duff, and Martina McBride. For each act's most recent release, the Fountains' *Out-of-State Plates* had sold 38,000 copies; Duff's 2005 compilation *Most Wanted* had sold 1.4 million copies; and McBride's *Timeless*, also released in 2005, had sold 1.2 million copies. No one would reasonably expect the Fountains' album to have generated the same volume of sales as big-name acts like Duff and McBride, and the Fountains' music certainly wasn't likely to appeal to the same demographic groups that loved those two singers. But the comparison of sales figures for each act's best-selling album was also somewhat sobering. The Fountains' best-selling album, *Welcome Interstate Managers*—which had a hit single to drive interest in it—had sold 427,000 copies; Duff's most popular album, 2003's *Metamorphosis*, had sold 3.9 million copies, and McBride's 2001 *Greatest Hits* album had sold 2.9 million. Those were the music business realities that the Fountains were up against.

The first single from *Traffic and Weather* was "Someone to Love." The video for the single was directed by Adam Neustadter, a friend of Adam and Jody's and a longtime fan of the band, who said that he envisioned the song as "two lonely characters living right next to each other in New York, but with no idea that the other exists." Comedians Demetri Martin and Faryl Millet played the roles of the two neighbors. Martin was a particularly inspired piece of casting to play Seth Shapiro who "got his law degree" since he had almost completed a law degree at New York University, dropping out in his final year to pursue a career in comedy. He and Millet, sitting in hyper-stylized tiny apartments, portrayed the daily routines of two people who, Neustadter said, "despite being so lonely, [are] still cutthroat New Yorkers who are too busy to care." The Fountains appeared in the video playing the song on the TV set that each character was watching in their respective apartments. Nonetheless, the single wasn't a hit, and neither was its follow-up, "'92 Subaru."

In the meantime, the *Cry-Baby* musical had gone through several lengthy rounds of development, with its producers staging several readings of the show to attract potential financial backers and theater bookers. Universal Pictures' theater division reportedly invested $12 million in the production. *Cry-Baby* finally had its live premiere in San Diego in November 2007, with a Broadway opening scheduled for the following spring. Adam told a Baltimore reporter covering the show's San Diego debut that writing songs for Fountains of Wayne had helped him write songs for *Cry-Baby*'s characters: "When I write for Fountains of Wayne, it might seem like I have an open slate, but actually

I don't. I always have in mind who will be singing the song and what his personality is." Nonetheless, both he and his co-writer David Javerbaum admitted they were relieved when *Cry-Baby* was "locked" a few days into the month-long San Diego run, after which no further changes could be made.

Adam and Chris both turned forty in October 2007. Adam and his wife Kate were now the parents of two young daughters, which had shifted his priorities. "I realized quickly that as soon as I pick up my guitar at home, my daughter tells me to put it down, so that's not good for business." And Chris was musing on the band's future direction. "I never would have thought we would have had a hit, but it's pretty confusing when you look at the pop charts right now. I don't know where we fit in."

10. JUST YOU WAIT

Fountains of Wayne ended their touring commitments for 2007 with a late October show in Honolulu. With *Traffic and Weather* completed and released, and nothing immediate on the band's schedule beyond three January 2008 shows in Spain, each of the band members temporarily focused their attentions elsewhere.

In February, Adam and Chris played together at a New York City fundraiser for PAX, an anti-gun-violence activist group. When a gunman opened fire at the top of the Empire State Building in February 1997, Adam's high school friend Matt Gross was shot in the head, and Chris Burmeister, the guitarist in Matt's band the Bushpilots, was killed. Matt survived but was now living with the after-effects of a traumatic brain injury. His brother, Dan, founded PAX to aid victims of gun violence and advocate for better gun control laws.

Cry-Baby started its Broadway previews in mid-March and officially opened on April 24. It received praise for its choreography and music; the *Baltimore Sun*'s theater critic, Mary Carole McCauley, who had also seen the show during its San Diego run, said that Adam and David's music "is so hummable that five months after hearing their melodies twice, I could replay three of their songs in my head." But most New York City critics, perhaps unfairly, compared *Cry-Baby* to its predecessor *Hairspray* and felt that *Cry-Baby* generally came up short. However, Adam was able to celebrate the ninety-seventh birthday of his grandfather—the former musical theater impresario—by taking him to a performance of his grandson's own Broadway musical.

The producers of *Cry-Baby* closed the show on June 22. It lost most of its substantial financial investment during its short run. Adam and David were nominated for a Tony Award for their musical score, but the award went to Lin-Manuel Miranda (who went on to create *Hamilton*) for *In the Heights*. Reflecting on the whole experience a few months after *Cry-Baby* shut down, Adam said, "Everything I work on is collaborative to a certain degree, but the way in which Broadway is collaborative is much more intense. There's always a better idea for something, and at a certain point it's hard to have any perspective when you've thought about something 18 different ways."

Adam and David already had their next gig lined up: something in the more familiar setting of television. They were composing the songs for a Christmas special starring Stephen Colbert, the archly right-wing blowhard—i.e., the archly right-wing blowhard named Stephen Colbert, played by the comedian Stephen Colbert—who hosted *The Colbert Report* on the Comedy Central cable TV channel. Colbert had known Adam since 1996, when Adam and Steven Gold wrote the music for ABC's short-lived series *The Dana Carvey Show*, in which Colbert was a cast member. "I had a clear, clear command to everyone involved with the show: no cynicism," Colbert told the Associated Press. "We're not mocking Christmas specials. We're doing MY Christmas special. That was the aesthetic we tried to bring into it."

Chris largely laid low, playing a few shows with the Gay Potatoes. In June, he was the opening act for a Northampton show by the band Campbell Apartment, which included his friend Ari Vais. "We love his music, he loves our music, and yes, he's famous," Vais told the local newspaper. "Having him open for us and not the other way around was strictly his idea."

In July, Jody released *Close to the Sun*, his first solo album. The songs on the album were written and recorded over several years. "Fountains of Wayne are great at writing stories about people they don't know. I thought I'd be less lyrically inclined to write about things I don't know about," he explained. "So I pulled from my personal experiences. Seventy-five percent is my point of view, and there is some of the stuff that may be about someone I know."

The Colbert special was filmed over three days in August, during which Adam and David got to see their seasonal songs performed by John Legend, Willie Nelson, Feist, Toby Keith, Elvis Costello, and Jon Stewart, David's former colleague at *The Daily Show*. Adam and David wrote a song specifically for each cast member—a task that challenged them to create music in a range of styles and for singers with widely varying levels of expertise. Adam told the *New York Times* that Willie Nelson had taken a few liberties with their composition when performing his song, but, he added, "Who am I to tell Willie Nelson how to sing a country song?"

In September, Adam and Chris performed at a benefit concert for Kelly Buchanan, a musician friend that Adam had previously collaborated with. Buchanan had been severely injured when a hockey puck hit her in the head; the resulting brain damage left her unable to speak or walk. The benefit featured musical guests playing songs from the album Buchanan had been working on, and raised money to support her recovery. The same month, Chris contributed a cover of his friend Mark Mulcahy's song "Cookie Jar" to *Ciao My Shining Star: The Songs of Mark Mulcahy*, an album that was a fundraiser for Mulcahy and his two daughters after the sudden death of Mulcahy's wife, Melissa.

The Colbert Christmas special aired in late November. That same month, Adam told *Billboard* that the next Fountains album was underway, with plans to release it in 2009. "We still have a way to go, but we have eight songs that are relatively close to complete now. We're looking to regroup after the New Year and do the second batch." He also mentioned that he was recording with Ivy for their next album. At the end of the year, L.L.Bean licensed "Valley Winter Song" for use in a Christmastime television commercial celebrating the joys of staying snuggly and warm indoors; Chris observed that this was ironic since the song was about wintertime depression.

After *Traffic and Weather* failed to match the (relative) success of *Welcome Interstate Managers*, Fountains of Wayne parted ways with Q Prime, their management firm, and with S-Curve, their record label. The band embarked on a tour in February 2009, but there was a significant difference between this Fountains tour and their previous outings; this time, they were touring as a largely acoustic act. Adam joked that the real reason for the tour was to get out of New York City during the winter, but the more serious motivation was to play new songs in front of live audiences, and to tour with lower costs. "We've done plenty of [acoustic] stuff like radio stations and gigs, but this tour is the very first one we've done in a van," he explained. "It's an interesting adjustment to make. We're in between records and we wanted to do something different. We don't have to bring a big crew and a lot of gear, and it's actually been really fun, a lot more conversational with the audience." Adam also mentioned that he and Chris had "about eight songs in progress, and we'll probably do another batch. We usually record a fair more than we need, and then we whittle it down."

"Acoustic" was a somewhat misleading description for these shows, as the Fountains had not eschewed electricity entirely. Adam played piano when the venue had one he could use, while Jody switched between electric and acoustic guitar, and filled in on bass as needed. Reviewers enjoyed the shows, with most commenting on how creatively the band's songs had been rearranged for the new minimalist format. "Stacy's Mom," for example, had been reimagined with what one reviewer described as "a cocktail-lounge feel, with jazzy noodling piano and brushed drums." Another observed that "the acoustic format brought out the plangent undercurrent in older songs such as 'Please Don't Rock Me Tonight,' and softened the places where the band's cutting observations sometimes shade into smug sarcasm." Somewhat tellingly, though, "Stacy's Mom" was only played as an encore. Among the new songs that made their way into the main sets were "A Road Song," "Cold Comfort Flowers," "Cemetery Guns," and "The Summer Place." "Every other time we went into the studio, we tried to get tape rolling before we lost interest in the song," Chris noted. "But this time, the arrangements [of the new songs] had a lot of time to change and grow on tour."

After the tour ended in late February, Adam made a

big announcement. He had already started writing songs for TV's *Sesame Street*, which he would continue to do off and on for several years—but now, as if being in two bands and doing other projects on the side wasn't enough, he was joining a third band. Tinted Windows was a power pop supergroup that, in addition to Adam on bass, included Taylor Hanson on keyboards and vocals, Adam's old friend James Iha on guitar, and drummer Bun E. Carlos from Cheap Trick. Adam and Taylor had known each other for more than a decade, having met when Adam and Hanson (the band) were put together by Hanson's management for a songwriting session. Nothing came of it, but Adam and Taylor stayed in touch, and in 2006 Adam suggested to him that they "do a power pop super combination of different musicians, and it just seemed like a fun idea." It took nearly three years to get all four band members in the same place long enough to record an album.

Tinted Windows made its live debut at the SXSW festival in Austin, Texas, in March. A reviewer from the *Chicago Sun-Times* described its set as "classic power-pop jangle with just a hint of bubblegum silliness . . . the new group played with bountiful exuberance and ample confidence—hardly a surprise, given all of the combined experience." Meanwhile, as if to remind the world that Fountains of Wayne were still a going concern, the hour-long concert the band filmed in Chicago in 2005 for PBS's *Soundstage* was released on DVD, with the title *No Better Place*. The sixteen-song set included most of the band's standard live favorites, with the addition of the rarely played "Janice's Party" from *Out-of-State Plates*. The DVD also included a bonus segment, recorded in the studio at the end of 2008, of the band performing acoustic versions of five songs.

And another, somewhat sadder, event occurred that same month. Fountains of Wayne—the store—closed its doors for good. In addition to giving the Fountains their name, the store had appeared in an episode of the New Jersey crime-and-much-more TV series *The Sopranos* and thus was now a pop-culture icon as well as a New Jersey icon. But despite having been in business for more than forty years, the store was no longer able to compete with newer big-box chain retailers that sold the same kinds of merchandise at lower prices. "Don Winters and everybody at the store were always really kind to us," Adam told the local newspaper, "and were tolerant of our shenanigans." At an auction later in the spring, fans of the store bought most of its inventory, including the figurines and decorations from the beloved Christmas displays.

The Fountains regrouped for a series of summer and early fall dates, with the occasional break in their schedule to accommodate Adam's commitments to perform with Tinted Windows. The self-titled Tinted Windows album had been released in April on S-Curve Records and received good reviews, but it was somewhat unclear what the band was planning to do next. Taylor Hanson told the *New York Times*, "We're not making any commitments officially [but] I definitely think there will be another record." Although Adam was the catalyst that brought Tinted Windows together, it was also unclear whether he intended to continue with that band as well as with the Fountains and with Ivy—although Ivy was now on an indefinite hiatus. They had started working on a new album in 2008 but became collectively dissatisfied with the results, and decided to put things on hold for a while. That also allowed Chase and Durand to focus on raising their two young children.

As the time between Fountains albums grew lengthier, the band members were inevitably asked why the next album was taking so long. "The main [reason] is just having enough songs that we like to release," Adam explained. "Also, I think that the slow pace that we've operated at is the reason that the band has lasted this long. I think that if we were doing an album a year, or even an album every two years, and touring in between, we would have probably stopped speaking to each other many years ago. I think that the space and the distance is necessary."

In July, Adam's work on the Colbert special was recognized with a nomination for a prime-time Emmy Award in the category of Outstanding Original Music and Lyrics, for the song "Much Worse Things." In September, the Fountains played a benefit concert at Glenfield Middle School in Montclair, which Adam had attended and which was now a magnet school for visual and performing arts students. The sold-out concert raised funds for the school's parent-teacher association to buy computers and printers for the school's classrooms, and two of Adam's former teachers joined the Fountains for a couple of songs.

But among all that activity, the Fountains were well aware that the music industry was evolving, and not necessarily in ways that favored the band's kind of music. In November, Adam and the band's lawyer, Josh Grier, visited Columbia Law School to give a presentation to students about the business side of the industry. Grier expressed the opinion that because of online file sharing, YouTube videos, increasingly narrowly focused radio playlists, and tough times for many record stores, artists could no longer rely on record labels to promote them. He said that the Fountains played live more often now "as a way to keep the music moving forward, to keep the fan base intact." Adam added, "A record deal doesn't have the cachet that it used to have."

Then, oddly enough, an opportunity for artists to repurpose their best-known songs ended up getting the Fountains some attention as well. The *MTV Unplugged* TV series featured artists playing stripped-down versions of their greatest hits, and when Katy Perry starred on an episode in November, the set list, much to everyone's surprise, included a cover of "Hackensack." "She's such an amazing singer, but she changed the whole thing around," Chris commented, referring to how Perry sang the verses an octave higher than the chorus—the opposite of how the Fountains had performed the song. "I don't know what possessed her to do that, but it's cool anyway."

At the start of 2010, the band entered Stratosphere Studios, with the goal of getting back to work and finishing the next album.

11. ANOTHER STATE OF MIND

Fountains of Wayne had been ignored by the Grammy Awards since the debacle of the Best New Artist nomination. But in February 2010, Adam got his own Grammy, as co-producer of the Colbert Christmas special soundtrack, which won the Best Comedy Album award. However, there were now more serious matters occupying his time. There wasn't a clear consensus within the band on the direction of the new album they were making. Adam wanted to continue with more pop-oriented songs; Chris, on the other hand, wanted to address more serious topics and grow the band beyond being known for humor. Part of Chris's motivation came from his experience of physical and mental recovery. He said that before his breakdown he had been "kind of going through the motions for a few years." But, he added, "the good thing about it is coming out of the other end of that and being able to sort of reassess what I want to do with the band—[being] more reflective of the person that I am and not trying to play up to what other people's idea of what the band is."

Arguments between Adam and Chris were a routine part of their joint creativity. Neal Robinson, a school friend of

Adam's from Montclair who reconnected with him when they were adults, said that "[Adam] was looking for his own personal John Lennon, and I think that's what he found in Chris. He would probably punch me in the face for saying that, but that's just the way their personalities interacted. And that's how they created art. Sometimes to create art you need conflict."

But now Adam's and Chris's clashes had become more intense. "We butted heads on this record," Chris told the *Boston Globe*, "a lot more than we did on any other record. There was a lot of fighting."

One dispute between them was over the line "*Between the stops at the Cracker Barrel/And forty movies with Will Ferrell*" in the lyrics of "A Road Song." Chris loved the song, but he didn't want to sing that particular line because "being funny didn't appeal to me anymore." Eventually he was persuaded to record the lyric as it was written, but, as he described it, "once you start having those sorts of disagreements, it turns into a power struggle." Another quarrel arose over Chris's song "Cemetery Guns," which presented the sadness of a military funeral as a commentary on the pointless losses of life during war. "At first we had a discussion, like, 'This doesn't belong on a Fountains of Wayne record,'" Chris recalled. "And I was like, Why the [expletive] not? You struggle with what your fans are expecting and who you might alienate by doing this. The answer always has to be, [expletive] it. Just make the record you want to make."

"We've known each other since we were eighteen," Adam reflected. "I don't feel closer musically to anybody else in the world. The two of us agree on about 99 percent of stuff, but when we butt heads, it gets pretty contentious." Adam having taken the lead on *Traffic and Weather* because of

Chris's health issues also indirectly caused problems as the new album took shape. "I had a lot of ideas that I wanted to get across," Chris told another interviewer, "and we hadn't been used to working in that relationship where each person was contributing equally to the project."

A few years later, Adam's close friend and Ivy bandmate Andy Chase made an observation about Adam's general working style that could also partly explain the vehemence of the conflicts Adam and Chris were experiencing. "Adam was a fiercely independent person. And that independence came at a price for his collaborators, because he was very consistent in having a vision for where he wanted to go and how he wanted to get there. It could often be a source of contention for people he collaborated with, because he was never not sure of anything. He dove into everything with 100% confidence. And because he was so talented and so smart and so funny, it almost always worked. But it took a very willful confident collaborator to successfully partner with that."

Adam's busy schedule was also a challenge in getting the Fountains' album completed. Indeed, in early 2010, Adam revealed that Ivy had also begun working on its next album. He characterized the Fountains as following the band's usual working pattern: "We tend to put out a record every three to four years, we do some touring, and then we get away from each other for a while." But he told a slightly different story to another writer. "We go [into the studio] for a couple of days and then don't do anything for six months. Partly it's the conflicting schedules. And then Chris tends to never be sure if he wants to do it any more between each record, until he decides that he does."

When Adam and Chris were jointly interviewed by *New*

York magazine, Chris joked that the Fountains "come close to breaking up" at least once a week, while Adam mused on how his and Chris's friendship had evolved. "We know each other so well, and that can be a great thing, and sometimes it can be a bad thing. When we're together, we have a great time. And then when we're all in different places, we'll get into email fights." However, things were becoming much more fractured within the group than anyone fully admitted at the time. Chris later revealed that his and Adam's arguments in the studio became so disruptive that they decided to stop the recording sessions, and sought professional help to mend their relationship. According to Chris, they "tried to work out a whole bunch of things that were going on between us." With the help of a psychiatrist, they reached an agreement. They would complete the album, go on tour to promote it after it was released, and then go their separate ways.

Jody later called the experience of making the album "our *Abbey Road.* It took me—if I don't mind patting myself on the ass—putting it back together. There were arguments going on between this and that, the legal eagles. It's like when you're breaking up with a girlfriend, but you don't actually do it, you just blame everyone. Have you done this before, my friend? It took you about three weeks to do it, didn't it? It took about six months to get [the album] ready to show the world."

In order to have enough time to work on the album, the band's touring activity during the first part of 2010 was minimal, mostly consisting of a trip to Japan in January and two New Jersey dates in May. Chris participated in some shows in and around Northampton, including a tribute concert of Alex Chilton's music, and a drop-in gig in Hartford, Connecticut, where he played a set of Ricky

Nelson songs. Adam played some shows with Mike Viola, performing songs that both of them had written for movies and other projects outside their own bands.

In the fall of 2010, the Fountains undertook another short tour, starting with a few dates in California but then mostly playing in the eastern US. In August, Taylor Hanson had suggested, during a tour to support Hanson's new album, that there was a "good chance" of another Tinted Windows album. But in October, Chris revealed that the new Fountains album had been completed and was being mastered. However, the band was still seeking a deal to release it. "If we end up shopping it around and don't get a major label to put it out, then it'll come out sooner, because we won't have to stay on their release schedule and put it out in the spring."

The album release turned out to be a little later than Chris had predicted. In April 2011, Yep Roc Records announced that in the fall it would be releasing *Sky Full of Holes*, Fountains of Wayne's fifth album. The announcement described the album as "simultaneously witty and wistful, imaginative and personal." Yep Roc, an independent label based in North Carolina, had been operating for fifteen years and had gradually become something of a home for well-regarded artists who, although they had dedicated fans, were not high-profile enough to be of interest to major labels focused on sales metrics and chart placements. The label described itself as "a rare sanctuary for the feeling of what it means to covet music and to cherish the chance to share it." Among the artists on Yep Roc's roster when Fountains of Wayne joined were Nick Lowe, Chatham County Line, Chris Stamey, and Scott McCaughey.

For the first time, however, there was a direct conflict

between a Fountains of Wayne record and one of Adam's other musical projects. In 2007, after Adam finished working with the band America on their *Here and Now* album, he remained friendly with guitarist/vocalist Gerry Beckley. In late 2009 America decided to make an album of cover versions of songs by artists whose music they liked, and Beckley asked Adam if there were any new Fountains of Wayne songs that he could use. Adam gently deflected the question at first but ended up sending Beckley a demo of "A Road Song." Beckley liked the song, but the Fountains had already recorded it for *Sky Full of Holes*. "I was actually really mad at Gerry," Adam said. "He said, 'Do you mind if we do this song?' I said, 'I don't mind, but could you wait until our version of it comes out at least, because we haven't released ours yet.' But then they just went ahead and did it anyway." The America album, *Back Pages*, came out in July, just ahead of *Sky Full of Holes'* release in August.

The cover of *Sky Full of Holes* was a far cry from the bright colors and strong graphics on the front of the Fountains' previous releases. The streamlined lowercase Fountains of Wayne logo was gone, replaced by the band name and album title in a loose handwritten font. The striking cover image, in musty shades of brown and green, was a diorama titled "Library," constructed and photographed by New York artists Lori Nix and Kathleen Gerber. It showed a tree growing toward a large hole in the roof of what appeared to be an abandoned multistory library. The series of artworks that included "Library" was described by the artists as "depict[ing] a future in which man-made environments have been emptied of human inhabitants and reclaimed by nature." Were the ruined library and the thin trees signs of a new beginning or a depiction of the rubble of an abandoned past? Or was it both?

The ambiguity of the cover, and the contrast of new growth and old artifacts in the cover image, reflected the mixture of songs on *Sky Full of Holes*. There was some of what Chris described as "the literal ones [which] are the easier ones to write," such as "A Dip in the Ocean" (written "all in one sitting, about riding around in a car with the top down"), and there were more abstract experiments such as "Cold Comfort Flowers," which emerged from "a bunch of notes I've collected, [because] sometimes a song can be a collection of ideas that all fit the same theme." Chris added, "I went through a pretty big phase of writing for this record, and as a result there are songs I've written that didn't even make the album." *Sky Full of Holes* sounded different—"We talked about making it a little more open and organic," Adam said, "with an emphasis on acoustic instruments and fewer tracks with wall-to-wall guitars"—and also sounded like the work of mature artists. The harried stressed-out dad of "Action Hero," dreaming of "*saving the world for all mankind*" while "*racing against time*," would likely not have been portrayed so empathetically earlier in the Fountains' career. "Hate to See You Like This" in some ways revisited the same topic as "She's Got a Problem" from their first album, but with new sensitivity in its stark portrayal of depression: "*Let's get your phone reconnected/Let's get this room disinfected.*" There were also inventive touches that made songs come alive, such as the staccato chords of "Acela" mimicking the rhythm of rolling train wheels, and the unresolved ending of "Workingman's Hands"—"*Now the old iron gate/Could use some fresh paint*"—evoking the never-ending tasks of manual labor.

But maturity perhaps also led to restraint. While the

Fountains were always capable of rocking hard, *Sky Full of Holes* felt like they were holding back a little; perhaps the conflicts over the direction of the album led them to be more subdued than before. Adam acknowledged that "we want to be able to evolve as a band. We want to be able to try different things. But I don't know if we're thinking in terms of maintaining a sound that we've already established. This record sounds fairly different from some of our other ones within the context of what we do, but it still sounds like the same band."

Critical assessments of *Sky Full of Holes* noticed the contrast between the more acoustic sound and the shimmering guitar-based power pop reminiscent of the band's previous work, along with the contrast between more serious songs and those with a more sardonic attitude. Not every critic felt that the album successfully navigated those contrasts. Steven Hyden in the *Chicago Tribune* described *Sky Full of Holes* an album of "adulthood, loaded with songs about middle-aged subjects, [and] using the mundane as a shield." Jim Farber, in the NY *Daily News*, expressed the concern that "the Fountains' words can outdistance their music," but said that the "small scale of the music, and the generous intent of the lyrics, give [the album] humanity and heart." Marc Hirsh in the *Boston Globe* called "Cemetery Guns" and "Hate to See You Like This" "majestic and stately," but also suggested that *Sky Full of Holes* continued the "identity crisis" of *Traffic and Weather*, saying that while the songs "offer up details galore, they never quite explain why we should care; it's like listening to a storyteller who doesn't skimp on the minutiae but never gets to the point."

Sky Full of Holes cracked the Top 40 album chart in the US, becoming Yep Roc's highest-placing album release that year.

A video was released for "The Summer Place"—although the setting looked like a traditional seaside town on the US East Coast, it was actually filmed in Bolinas, California—but "Richie and Ruben" became the first single, without a video to accompany it. That was a shame, as the entrepreneurial disasters of the song's title characters would have made for engaging visuals. The second single, "Someone's Going to Break Your Heart," had a rather conventional "blurry life on tour" video, not completely relevant to the lyrics of the song. The video for "A Road Song," with its black-and-white footage of the band traveling and performing, was much more effective. But by this time, the influence of MTV and other music video outlets had decreased. Videos were still a viable way to promote an album or single, but the success of a video was no longer going to make or break a band or a record, as it had in the past.

While the Fountains were busy launching *Sky Full of Holes*, Tinted Windows seemed to be gearing up for more activity. In May, Bun E. Carlos had said that Tinted Windows would be "returning to the studio in the near future" to make its second album, and in August Taylor Hanson said there was some "brewing tunage" between him and Adam for the next album. But with the various commitments of all four of the band's members, getting together to write or record was as challenging as it had been before, and nothing substantial emerged.

The Fountains spent much of 2012 on tour, with some breaks in late September and October so that Adam could play shows with Ivy to promote that band's album *All Hours*. Philip Brasor, an American writer living in Japan, attended a Fountains show in Tokyo in March and made some sharp observations about the band's performance, noting the lack of songs from *Sky Full of Holes* in their set. "Their tunes seem custom made for singalongs and just sound plain good in a live setting. [But] there's no particular reason why the group has to play pretty much the same set list it has for the past decade. Cult bands should understand that anything they do is going to be acceptable, and obscure stuff may be even more appreciated. I wish they had approached their excitable Tokyo fans as real friends, rather than just another audience. They don't need to be won over."

The band returned to Japan in July to play the huge outdoor Fuji Rock Festival, which they had performed at several times in the past. That year the festival was staged partly as a benefit for emergency relief, as Japan had experienced a major earthquake earlier in the year. During the summer, Brian joined the Jesus and Mary Chain for part of their reunion tour in the US. In October, the Fountains appeared on NPR Music's *Tiny Desk Concert* video series, playing a four-song set ("The Summer Place," "Valley Winter Song," "A Dip in the Ocean," and "Troubled Times") with Chris and Jody on acoustic guitar, Adam alternating between acoustic guitar and bass, and Brian on a single snare drum. Many fans felt that the minimalist format demonstrated the brilliance of the Fountains' songs, in not needing a lot of instrumentation or studio effects to be compelling, and considered this one of the band's best live performances. In the first two weeks of November, the Fountains swung through continental Europe and the UK.

Adam told *Billboard* that the band hadn't yet decided whether there would be a follow-up to *Sky Full of Holes*. He noted that Chris had been talking about making a solo album, "but then again he may decide that those songs will end up on a Fountains record. If we each start writing it may be the kind of thing where if we have three, four songs each we'll get excited about starting something new. But we haven't had one discussion yet." It was telling that Adam, generally positive and upbeat during interviews, was now publicly alluding to the conflict within the band, such as saying that "tak[ing] time to get away from each other doesn't hurt." He also mentioned that the members of Tinted Windows wanted to keep the band going, but only "[i]f we can get everyone to commit to a week or two, somewhere. [Then] maybe another album will get made."

Yep Roc rereleased *Utopia Parkway* on vinyl—a treat for Fountains fans, since the original release was on CD and cassette—and all the band members played on comedian/ actor Harry Shearer's album *Can't Take a Hint*, backing him up on the track "Celebrity Booze Endorser."

In September, Adam won an Emmy Award for "It's Not Just for Gays Anymore," the original song he and David Javerbaum wrote for the opening of the 65th Tony Awards broadcast. He and Steven Gold also took on the job of arranging versions of current hit songs, and writing the occasional original song, for a new TV series, *Wedding Band*, about the adventures of a (fictional) cover band that played at wedding receptions. "It just seemed like a good idea for a show, and it seemed like a fun idea," he said, although he also admitted that it was "a ton of work."

In October, the Fountains played at Yep Roc's twenty-fifth anniversary celebration concert, and in December, they appeared with Harry Shearer at his live Christmas Without Tears show in New York City. At the end of 2012, they began preparing for what would turn out to be their final live shows.

12. EVOLVE IN TIME

"We're starting to think about writing some more songs," Adam said in March 2013, "and maybe making another record." The Fountains played a set of shows that month in the eastern and central US, including a date in Morristown, New Jersey, that had been postponed from the previous December because of Hurricane Sandy. They also went into Stratosphere Studio to record one last song together: "Trucks," a track that appeared on *Frog Trouble*, a CD by children's author and illustrator Sandra Boynton. Boynton and her musical collaborator Michael Ford wrote the rollicking country song, which cleverly shifted through key changes as it described the joys of driving and the open road. The *Frog Trouble* CD was released with an illustrated songbook that included sheet music for all the songs "because," Boynton said, "the making of music and the making of recordings is something I would love children and people to think about a little bit."

The evolution of online technology was starting to generate new opportunities for musicians. In early summer, Adam undertook his first job writing music for an online-only streaming show. He and David Javerbaum wrote two songs for the pilot episode of *Browsers*, a musical comedy series on Amazon Prime about a group of interns working for an online news site. "This model [of streaming shows] is an experiment," Adam said, "but it's an interesting one." Jody, for his part, launched an online Kickstarter campaign in June to fund the creation of his next solo album. "I've recorded in big studios with major label budgets in the past, but the music industry has changed over the last several years," he wrote on the site. "With today's technology, I could probably record 95% of this in a Barnes & Noble bathroom, but I've decided to bring it to Kickstarter to get funding so I can put out a proper product." The campaign met its goal of $22,000 by the end of July, and Jody headed into his studio to work on the album, writing all the songs and playing almost all the instruments himself.

The Fountains returned in September and October for another series of shows, with Evan Dando and Soul Asylum as opening acts. The final show of that brief tour—October 19, at First Avenue in Minneapolis—was the last live show that Adam, Chris, Jody, and Brian would play together as Fountains of Wayne.

In addition to continuing to work with Ivy, Adam collaborated with the pop duo Fever High, co-writing and producing their debut EP and eventually their first album. Michael Krumper, who was involved in publicizing the album, described Fever High as "a high-concept duo where Adam wrote songs for two female vocalists, writing retro-pop that paired Bananarama's flat affect vocals with nineties dance pop." Adam also won another Emmy Award, along with a Writers Guild of America Award, for "If I Had Time," the song he wrote to close out the 66th Tony Awards broadcast. The song's lyrics lamented not having enough time to recap the show, and the song was hilariously cut off in the middle of a line as the broadcast ended.

Brian had now become a full-time member of the Jesus and Mary Chain, which would occupy his time for most of the coming decade. Jody's crowdfunded album, *Month of Mondays*, was released in the spring of 2014. Chris kept himself busy that year playing the occasional solo show and participating in various projects with his Northampton musician friends. He contributed covers of the Dream Academy's "Life in a Northern Town" and Gordon Lightfoot's "Sundown" to compilation albums. And on the side, he became an Uber driver. "It's a good way to meet people," he explained. He continued doing that until his car got too old to meet Uber's vehicle requirements.

Then in 2015, Adam embarked on the project that was to dominate his work for several years: the CW network's TV series *Crazy Ex-Girlfriend*. The show chronicled the romantic and professional life of Rebecca Bunch, a lawyer who dumped a promising career in New York to move to California on the very faint chance of reconnecting with an ex-boyfriend. In each episode the show's characters regularly burst out into song and dance, with the musical numbers fully staged and choreographed like a Broadway musical or a music video. The songs were all original, and every episode had at least two of them; Rachel Bloom, the show's co-creator and star, described the music as the "emotional tent poles" of the show.

Bloom co-wrote the songs with Adam and her other collaborator, Jack Dolgen. Adam and Steven Gold also took on the roles of music producers for the series, which required working with "[anything] from synthesizers and drum machines to a 19-piece orchestra." Not only did the songwriters and producers create, record, and stage each song, they also regularly released "dirty" versions of songs on the internet, when the CW "standards and practice" censors deemed certain lyrics unacceptable for broadcast. While Adam had learned from his work on musicals, TV shows, and movies how to write songs for specific characters and storylines, he was unaccustomed to writing that many songs that quickly. Aline Brosh McKenna, the co-creator of the show, said that Adam once told her, "The only person who thought this was possible was you, because you're not a musician or a songwriter." She added, "If I had been, I would have known what it really meant to write two or three songs each week. It was relentless."

Adam's work appeared on Broadway again when he co-wrote a song for David Javerbaum's comedy *An Act of God*, which opened in May 2015 and ran throughout the summer. Adam also became one of the founding partners of Sid Gold's Request Room, a piano karaoke bar in New York City's Chelsea neighborhood that opened in the summer and became known as a nightspot that genuinely welcomed everyone from enthusiastic amateur singers to musical theater stars.

Adam and David's first musical collaboration was also immortalized by a very unusual CD release. Some cast members of the 2008 Broadway production of *Cry-Baby* felt that the show's music was so outstanding that it should be recorded for posterity, even though the show itself had been a flop. With the help of the Broadway Records label, "88.4% of the original Broadway cast" (according to the CD cover) reunited in the summer of 2015 to make a soundtrack album for the *Cry-Baby* musical. The album was proudly released seven years after the show itself closed.

But regardless of what each individual member of Fountains of Wayne got up to, they were regularly asked: Will there be another album? Are you going to work together again? It must have been irritating for the band members to repeatedly get those questions, but their answers were polite—and consistent. In a joint interview in 2016, Adam and Chris made it pretty clear that the chances of the band reuniting were small, at best. "If we can find a way to work together and have fun and be creative again and not have it be miserable, I'm totally into it. But I'm too old to have band fights," Adam said. "On *Sky Full of Holes*, we spent more time fighting than recording," said Chris. "I try never to say never, but it's staggering to think of everything that would have to happen for me to want to repeat that experience." Michael Krumper, for one, thought that was a shame. "I was honestly frustrated," he later recalled, "that neither could see clear to giving Fountains one more shot."

In July 2016, Look Park, a band that Chris had put together, released a self-titled album on Yep Roc. The band and album took their name from a park in Northampton, which itself was named after the family that donated the funds to build the park. Chris was joined on *Look Park* by Davey Faragher on bass and Michael Urbano on drums; Faragher and Urbano had previously played together in Cracker and in John Hiatt's touring band. Producer Mitchell Froom—who was also an alumnus of the Hill School, having graduated several years before Chris was a student there—played keyboards. All of *Look Park*'s songs had been written by Chris during the turbulent sessions for *Sky Full of Holes* and were recorded in Los Angeles at Froom's home studio. The album's graceful retro cover design was by Shepard Fairey, who in addition to having been a schoolmate of Jody's was also a friend of Froom's. Chris, an enthusiastic photographer who was fascinated by artistic design and composition, spent an afternoon hanging out in Fairey's studio and brainstorming ideas for the cover with him. "I told him I wanted it to feel like stepping into a garden," he said. "It's definitely different from what I had imagined, but it's fantastic."

When promoting *Look Park*, Chris was careful to specify that this was not a solo album, in the sense of being a side project from Fountains of Wayne. He wanted to establish a distinct identity for Look Park, and to that end he deliberately chose songs for the album that he thought did not sound like Fountains songs. He also made it clear that Look Park was not just Chris Collingwood. "It's band music," Chris said, "and I thought it should have a band name." His Northampton friend Philip Price, who played guitar for Look Park's live shows, said, "I'm not sure that as a songwriter Chris was trying to do anything radically different, but the production [on the album] is definitely more soulful. [And] ever since I met him, Chris has been looking for an escape hatch from Fountains of Wayne."

Nonetheless, when Look Park performed live, the set list generally included at least a few Fountains songs—"Red Dragon Tattoo," "Barbara H.," "Valley Winter Song," "A Dip in the Ocean," and "Survival Car." They also occasionally covered other artists' songs, such as World Party's "Put the Message in the Box" and Tom Petty and the Heartbreakers' "Breakdown." Look Park's live debut was a July 2016 gig at the Parlor Room in Northampton. They then flew to Japan to play the Fuji Rock Festival. After a late August performance at Amaurosaurus, a festival hosted by the band Lake Street Dive at the actual Look Park, the band toured the US throughout September and October. *Look Park* got solid reviews, although some writers seemed to struggle with whether to compare it to a Fountains of Wayne album. It wasn't an unreasonable association, but it seemed that not everyone could assess Look Park's music on its own merits.

Adam, meanwhile, produced a new album by the Monkees. *Good Times!*, released in May 2016 and also featuring contributions by Jody and Brian, was the band's first new album in twenty years. *Good Times!* combined updated recordings of unreleased songs from the band's commercial peak in the 1960s—"when they had the greatest songwriters in the world writing for them," according to Adam—and new songs written for the band by their modern-day fans, including Adam, who composed "Our Own World." "It was a blast," Adam said, "probably the most fun I've ever had making a record."

In July 2017, the band's friend Mike Denneen unexpectedly passed away. Denneen had supported and encouraged Fountains of Wayne after they had been dumped by Atlantic, and gave them the studio time in Boston that allowed them to create, and be successful with, *Welcome Interstate Managers*. Look Park continued to play live dates throughout the year, and Jody released another solo album, *Pacifier*. In the fall, Adam made a return to Williams College, where he was presented with the school's Bicentennial Medal—an annual award honoring "distinguished achievement" by alumni—for his accomplishments in music.

In 2018, Adam recruited Jody and Brian to play on another Monkees album, *Christmas Party*; in addition to producing it, he collaborated with novelist Michael Chabon to write the track "House of Broken Gingerbread." Adam also went on tour as part of Crazy Ex-Girlfriend Live, a series of concerts where cast members of the TV show performed songs from the show.

The final episode of *Crazy Ex-Girlfriend* aired in April 2019. Over the show's four-season run, Adam, Rachel Bloom, and Jack Dolgen had written nearly 150 original songs and won an Emmy Award for their music for the season finale. In May and June 2019, Chris was part of Songs and Stories, a six-week acoustic tour organized by Art Alexakis of Everclear that also featured John Wozniak of Marcy Playground and Max Collins of Eve 6. Each participant played some of their own band's songs, as well as playing several songs together and answering questions from the audience. Chris's set usually started with a cover of R.E.M.'s "(Don't Go Back to) Rockville," and in addition to five songs from the Fountains' repertoire, included Look Park's "You Can Come Round If You Want To."

At the end of 2019, Chris participated for the first time in Joey's Song, an annual benefit concert for childhood epilepsy research that he would continue to support in the coming years. The concert that year was in Madison, Wisconsin, and while there Chris also sat in with his friend Butch Vig's band the Know-It-All Boyfriends at a fundraiser to restore the Temple Theatre marquee in Vig's hometown of Viroqua.

13. UNWELCOME FATE

The year 2020 was terrible in many ways.

In January the COVID-19 virus started to spread around the globe, overwhelming health-care systems, causing millions of deaths, and closing businesses and services worldwide. Among the restrictions put in place to control the pandemic were bans on large gatherings in enclosed spaces—like live concerts. Musicians whose incomes relied on touring or performing suddenly lost those sources of revenue, and since recording studios also closed down, making and releasing new music was also impossible for many of them.

At the start of the year, it was announced that Adam and Rachel Bloom would be writing the songs for a new musical based on Fran Drescher's TV series *The Nanny*. Adam had also been working on another musical with comedian Sarah Silverman, an adaptation of her memoir *The Bedwetter*; that show was scheduled to debut off-Broadway in May. Live theater in New York shut down in mid-March. It was unclear whether rehearsals for *The Bedwetter* would start on March 17 as planned. Nonetheless, on March 12 Adam and the rest of the show's creative team went ahead with an already scheduled get-together and had a pizza-and-wine-fueled read-through of the show's entire script.

Adam and his wife Kate had divorced in 2013, and while Adam maintained an apartment in New York City, he had moved to a house in upstate New York with his girlfriend Alexis Morley. On March 15, Adam and Alexis went for a long walk outdoors. The next morning, Adam woke up with a fever. He spent the next few days resting at home with Alexis caring for him. Both of them thought that he had nothing more than a "crappy flu." But his condition worsened, and on March 23 she took him to the nearest hospital. Because of COVID-19 restrictions, Alexis wasn't allowed to go into the hospital building with Adam, but after she returned home, they chatted via text and he told her he loved her. The next day he was moved into the COVID-19 treatment ward and intubated. "I never got to hear his voice again," Alexis wrote.

The hospital staff in the COVID-19 ward were able to hold a cell phone to Adam's ear, so his family members and friends could talk to him even though he could not respond. The Fountains' lawyer, Josh Grier, issued a public statement that Adam was "very sick and heavily sedated, as are all people on ventilators." During the next few days, his condition showed some signs of improvement, although increasingly serious concerns were being expressed on social media. By now, most people were familiar with the usual progress of COVID-19 cases, and knew that a patient being very sick in the hospital for more than a few days was not a good sign.

During the evening of March 31, in Adam's mother's words, "it went to hell in a handbasket." In the middle of the night, Alexis got a call from the hospital, letting her know that Adam "wasn't going to make it." She raced over to the hospital, and after some negotiations with staff and donning "layers of protective equipment," she was allowed into the COVID-19 ward to spend an hour sitting by Adam's bedside. She described him as looking "sweet, peaceful, beautiful" although he was by then unconscious.

Just after Alexis arrived back home on the morning of April 1, a nurse from the COVID-19 ward called to tell her that Adam had passed peacefully. At that moment, she wrote, "the sun came out for a few minutes and lit up the entire sky."

During that week, the music world lost Ellis Marsalis Jr., Joe Diffie, Bucky Pizzarelli, Hal Willner, and John Prine to complications from COVID-19. More than 7,500 people in the US and 39,000 people worldwide died of COVID-19 complications in that same time. But Adam's death hit particularly hard, because of his relatively young age, everything that he had accomplished, and the awful randomness of it all. "I am feeling a bit lost here without him; as much as I grounded him, he grounded me and I feel like a typesetter's tray that has been spilled across the floor. And I don't understand any of this," wrote his lifelong friend Jeremy Freeman. "It all seems cheap and perverse and meaningless that one cough, one rubbed nose and I have lost my best friend; and I can't help but see the universe as wrong, skewed and slapped out of orbit that I will have to be 52 and 53 and so on and so on and Adam will always be 52."

Almost every tribute to Adam included positive quotes from his collaborators, among them Tom Hanks, Sarah Silverman, and Kathy Griffin. "He wrote the theme song to my talk show," Griffin recalled on Twitter. "He was so patient with me as I recorded it in the booth, guiding me at every step. He did the gig as a favor, in a little home studio on a Saturday." Fans from all walks of life expressed their sorrow, including producer and musician Jack Antonoff, who elegantly described Adam as "taking pop music to its classiest and most untouchable place." Even those who remembered occasionally being irritated by his stubbornness and drive were careful to point out that those characteristics were more than balanced out by his unassuming nature, his loyalty, his sense of humor, his wholehearted commitment to everything he undertook, and the deep affection they felt for him.

Rachel Bloom had a particularly difficult experience with her close friend's death. At the same time Adam was in the COVID-19 unit in a hospital on the East Coast, she was in a Los Angeles hospital after giving birth to her first child, a daughter, who had to spend several days in neonatal intensive care because of fluid buildup on her lungs. "Having a baby in the NICU during a pandemic while a dear friend was in the hospital 3,000 miles away made this by far the most emotionally intense week of mine and [her husband's] lives," she wrote. Adam died just after Bloom and her daughter were able to return home.

Chris issued a statement on Twitter on April 3, thanking everyone for their support, and expressing his condolences to Adam's children and parents. A week later he gave an interview to *Rolling Stone* in which he recalled meeting Adam at college, described how their relationship developed, and reflected on their experiences in Fountains of Wayne. "There were a lot of things I took for granted in FOW that I assumed all other bands had, but have since learned are rare," he said. "All four of us could play pretty much any song just by hearing it." He described Adam as "viewing himself as a craftsman and not an artist, a word he considered pretentious. He worked diligently every day, even when he didn't feel like it, which is true of a lot of successful people, and probably the greatest single difference between us."

The actors who played the Wonders, the band whose story was told in *That Thing You Do!*, reunited online on April 17 for a virtual watch-along party of the film, to pay tribute to Adam and to raise money for MusiCares, a charity that supports musicians in need—a particularly appropriate choice when so many musicians were financially struggling. A few days later, on April 22, Chris, Jody, and Brian reunited virtually as Fountains of Wayne to participate in a televised concert titled *Jersey 4 Jersey*. The concert was organized by Tammy Murphy, the wife of New Jersey's governor, to benefit the New Jersey Pandemic Relief Fund. Fellow Jerseyite Sharon Van Etten filled in on bass and backing vocals, with each of the four musicians playing in their own home.

Chris introduced the Fountains' segment by saying, "This is for Adam, his parents, his children, and New Jersey." Their performance of "Hackensack" was beautiful yet heartbreaking; it was poignant to see Chris, Brian, and Jody playing without Adam, and to realize there was now a hole in Fountains of Wayne that could never be filled. "That was a real hardship to do, because everybody was tucked into their lairs, and I didn't have a tripod," Jody said later. "It wasn't done all at once; it was done as a recording. So when you saw us on that show, it was phoning it in to some degree. You can see dirty laundry in the back of mine. They had candles and stuff lit on the other screens. Adam would've expected it out of me." The concert raised nearly $6 million in donations.

In June, a group of Adam's musical friends and admirers got together (virtually) to create *Saving for a Custom Van*, a tribute album for Adam released on Bandcamp. In addition to an original track by Jody, "Four in the Morning," it featured covers of songs from Fountains of Wayne, Ivy, and *Crazy Ex-Girlfriend*, as well as covers of "Way Back into Love" from *Music and Lyrics* and "Come On" from *Josie and the Pussycats*.

In spring 2021, when limited in-person gatherings were once again possible, Jody organized an incredible event: *Adam Schlesinger, a Music Celebration*. The two-hour show was recorded at the Bowery Electric venue in NYC and streamed online May 5, with proceeds from the online viewing going to MusiCares and to the venue. The performances, both in-person and taped, covered music from Adam's entire career. Mike Viola showed off the original "That Thing You Do!" cassette made by "Scientist Alexis" and performed the song with a group of friends that included an uncredited Brendon Urie of Panic! at the Disco on bass. Butch Walker performed "Guitar Center," an unreleased song written by Adam. The three remaining members of Tinted Windows reunited to perform "Back with You," and there were two versions each of "Hackensack" (Ben Lee and Glenn Tilbrook) and "That Thing You Do!" (the aforementioned Mike Viola and friends, and Bambi Kino). Interspersed with the musical numbers were appearances by Adam's friends and collaborators, including Jody, Mickey Dolenz, Harry Shearer, Drew Carey, and Sarah Silverman, sharing their memories of him. It was both a very enjoyable night of entertainment and a heartfelt tribute to a beloved musician and friend. "I did feel at times like John Phillips must have felt in booking Monterey," Jody said of the challenges he navigated in putting the show together. "But it was all worth it, and totally cathartic to me. There was no funeral, so it had to be done. I was pretty damn pleased with how it turned out."

Most venues and theaters around the world remained partially or fully closed until the summer of 2021. Reopenings were gradual, and performers had to deal with varying restrictions on audience capacity and social distancing. Some venues never recovered financially from the extended shutdown and ended up closing forever. The live music industry as a whole also struggled to recover, as musicians, audiences, and support staff adapted to the new realities of a post-pandemic world. And amid it all, the Fountains fans who had hoped for new music or more concerts had to accept that with Adam gone, Fountains of Wayne, as they knew them, had ended.

EPILOGUE: SHINE ON, SHINE ON, SHINE ON

Post-2020, Chris, Jody, and Brian all pursued their own musical paths. Jody released a solo album, *Waterways*, in 2023, co-produced by Brian and with Brian playing on several tracks; he also released a series of EPs online, most recently *Sunflowers, Vol. 1* in December 2024. Brian operated a recording studio in Los Angeles and continued to make guest appearances on other artists' records. Chris performed "Just a Few of My Friends," a new song by Sandra Boynton and Michael Ford, on Boynton's Christmas CD *Cows and Holly*, released in October 2024. Photos of Chris, Brian, and Jody together occasionally popped up on social media.

Adam's last major project, the musical *The Bedwetter*, opened off-Broadway in April 2022 for a three-month run. Adam was also commemorated in Rachel Bloom's one-woman musical play *Death, Let Me Do My Show*, based on her experiences during the week that Adam died. The show played on Broadway in fall 2023 and was filmed for a Netflix special released in fall 2024. It's unclear how much work was completed on *The Nanny* musical that Adam and Rachel were hired to write, but co-producer Fran Drescher stated in spring 2022 that the show was still moving forward.

Ivy's album *Long Distance* was reissued on vinyl in 2024 to mark its twenty-fifth anniversary, with the addition of "All I Ever Wanted," a previously unreleased track from the original album sessions. It has been rumoured that Andy Chase and Dominique Durand are working on a new Ivy album, using archived and unfinished songs that they had previously written or recorded with Adam.

Then, just as this book was going to press, something incredible happened. Fountains of Wayne announced that it would play several live shows in the summer of 2025, with Chris, Jody, and Brian joined by Steven Gold on keyboards and Max Collins on bass. Max had performed with Jody and with Chris in the past, and is a longtime power pop aficionado and Fountains admirer. Some Fountains followers griped that the band could never be the same without Adam, but most of the band's fans were completely thrilled that Fountains of Wayne was going to play live again. Representatives for the band also let it be known that Adam's family had given their approval for the shows to go ahead.

The ecstatic reaction to the announcement demonstrated the ongoing love for Fountains of Wayne. After Adam passed, there were some powerful testimonials to the lasting impact of the band's music. Michael Krumper said, "Fountains of Wayne's five albums stand as one of the strongest catalogs of songs by a band in the last quarter-century." Ken Weinstein recalled that "from the first chords of 'Radiation Vibe' . . . I knew we were in the presence of greatness. Twelve songs of pure power pop bliss that led to five more albums of pure joy, start to finish."

Ty Burr, in the *Boston Globe*, described the Fountains' songs as "rock-solid nuggets of rock and power pop that nod benevolently at the retro Top 40 cheese that filled car radios in the seventies and eighties while telling tales of suburbia that are alternately funny and moving." The *New Yorker*'s Jody Rosen suggested that "if future investigators want to understand the aspirations and setbacks of a certain kind of early twenty-first-century middle-class American white person, the [Fountains] songbook will be a benchmark text. What they'll find there, alongside the jokes and details, is deep human sympathy." Elizabeth Snyder of the *Kenosha News* remembered attending an outdoor Fountains concert in Milwaukee in 2004 on "a dark and stormy night" and standing completely rain-soaked with "a scant handful of people" in front of the stage. "They did not disappoint. Despite the sheets of rain coming down, they performed. I stood on the front bench, dead center, locking eyes with them, and it felt like they sang every tune just for me. That was, and remains, the greatest concert I have ever experienced."

In April 2020, Oregon newspaper columnist Les Gehrett suddenly had lots of time to listen to the Fountains' music when, as a cost-cutting measure, his employer placed him on two weeks' unpaid furlough—a situation that could have come straight out of the band's many songs about petty bosses and incomprehensible workplace decisions. Nonetheless, he came up with a near-perfect description of why the Fountains are a great band. "Fountains of Wayne," he wrote, "isn't a party band. It is a band for people who didn't get invited to the party, or who got stuck in traffic on the way to the party, or for those who managed to make it to the party but then spent the whole night sitting in a corner."

Now, the live performances by this new version of the band may be the catalyst that reintroduces Fountains of Wayne to the world. The Fountains have their long-time fans, but there's no reason why a new generation of listeners wouldn't love the band too. They might discover the Fountains through a friend, through a streaming service, through a random find in a record store, or through an online "Recommended for You" prompt—and now, they might go to a festival or venue and suddenly hear some tremendous songs they've never heard before. All they need is a push in the right direction. Fountains of Wayne's music is all out there, just waiting to be discovered and appreciated all over again.

ACKNOWLEDGMENTS

Chris Collingwood, Jody Porter, and Brian Young were not available to be interviewed for this book. My goal, as an external observer, was to tell the Fountains of Wayne story as honestly and respectfully as possible from that perspective. I hope that one day Chris, Jody, and Brian will decide to tell their stories themselves.

I relied on many secondary sources for the information in this book, including Newspapers.com, YouTube, ProQuest, World Radio History, and other article databases, podcasts, and online resources. A special shout-out goes to the anonymous curator of the Chris Collingwood Fan Club site on WordPress. That site's archives contain many articles that are no longer available anywhere else on the internet.

Jeff Gomez, the founder and publisher of J-Card Press, initiated this project by sending me a list of band names and asking which one interested me the most. "Fountains of Wayne" jumped out at me immediately. I'm very grateful to Jeff for his confidence in my work, and for the vision, planning, and organization that he brings to J-Card, all of which have been extremely helpful to me. Thanks also to Carrie Wicks for her meticulous copyediting and proofreading.

My mother, Carol, and my brother, Michael, are always supportive of my writing adventures, and I appreciate that very much.

The members of my Wednesday songwriting group never failed to ask how the book was going and were genuinely interested in its progress. That kept my spirits up during the difficult parts. Thank you, my friends: Mark Eliasof, Steven Campbell, Greg Antoniono, James Noble, Andy Hoffman, and Leslie Goldman.

My husband, Tom Barrett, was extremely tolerant of the many late nights and long weekends I spent in what we came to call "Fountains-land." He also used his superb editing and proofreading skills to make the manuscript much better than it would have been otherwise. I love you every day.

CHAPTER NOTES

Epigraph
Takiff, Jonathan. "The Word for the Weekend: Alternative; Nellie McKay, Fountains of Wayne Want to Stand Out from the Crowd." *Philadelphia Daily News*, July 16, 2004.

1. Two of a Kind
Freeman, Jeremy. "The Unfathomable Reality of Loss: Adam Schlesinger, 1967–2020." Oishi Gevalt, April 8, 2020. https://oishigevalt.com/2020/04/08/the-unfathomable-reality-of-loss-adam-schlesinger-1967-2020/.

Wise, Brian. "Eclectic Sounds of New Jersey, Echoing from Coast to Coast." *New York Times*, February 8, 2004.

Barber, Simon, and Brian O'Connor, hosts. Interview with Adam Schlesinger. *Sodajerker* (podcast), episode 58. Posted February 10, 2014. https://www.sodajerker.com/episode-58-adam-schlesinger/.

Goudreau, Chris. "Famed Musician Dies at 52." *Valley Advocate*, April 9, 2020.

"Library Presents Free Rock Concert." *Montclair Times*, June 20, 1985.

Williams, Joe. "Tell Me About That Song: Chris Collingwood, Vocalist of Power-Pop Band Fountains of Wayne." *Seattle Weekly*, September 11, 2011.

Paiva, Derek. "Wayne's World All About Music, Lyrics." *Honolulu Advertiser*, October 19, 2007.

Collingwood, Chris. "The Warm Thrill of Confusion." *New York Times*, August 16, 2013. https://archive.nytimes.com/opinionator.blogs.nytimes.com/2013/08/16/the-warm-thrill-of-confusion/.

Jenkins, Mark. "Fountains Flow into Utopia." *Washington Post*, July 2, 1999. https://www.washingtonpost.com/archive/lifestyle/1999/07/02/spotlight/098ce4eb-d0e7-4e39-90af-674db7d2e265/.

"Fountains of Wayne Gushes." *Chicago Tribune*, July 21, 2003. https://www.chicagotribune.com/2003/07/21/fountains-of-wayne-gushes/.

Darnell, Steve. "First Person: Chris Collingwood." *Chicago Tribune*, July 9, 1999.

Hoskyns, Barney. Fountains of Wayne (audio interview), January 24, 1997. https://www.rocksbackpages.com/Library/Article/fountains-of-wayne-1997.

Gross, Terry. Interview with Adam Schlesinger and Chris Collingwood. *Fresh Air*, NPR. Originally broadcast 1999; rebroadcast April 3, 2020. https://www.npr.org/2020/04/03/826654716/fresh-air-remembers-fountains-of-wayne-co-founder-adam-schlesinger.

Reisman, M. "Frosh Shine in Tribute to First-Year Woes and Joys." *Williams Record*, October 27, 1987.

Vozick-Levinson, Simon. "Melody and Mischief: How Adam Schlesinger Built a Songwriting Career Like No Other." *Rolling Stone*, April 10, 2020. https://www.rollingstone.com/music/music-features/adam-schlesinger-life-death-obituary-981333/.

2. The Ups and Downs, the Highs and Lows

Barber, Simon, and Brian O'Connor, hosts. Interview with Adam Schlesinger. *Sodajerker* (podcast), episode 58. Posted February 10, 2014. https://www.sodajerker.com/episode-58-adam-schlesinger/.

Catlin, Roger. "Local Flavor Flows Through Fountains' Pop." *Hartford Courant*, May 20, 1999.

Krumper, Michael. "Remembering Adam Schlesinger: A Tribute to a Friend." *Flood*, April 15, 2020. https://floodmagazine.com/76966/

remembering-adam-schlesinger-a-tribute-to-a-friend/.

Guzmán, Isaac. "Singing the Lives of Average Teen Guys." *Newsday*, November 11, 1999.

Meeting: Mahan, Rich, host. *The Rhino Podcast*, "Tribute to Adam Schlesinger" (part II). Posted May 13, 2020. https://www.rhino.com/ podcast/tribute-to-adam-schlesinger-with-rachel-bloom-ivy-fever-high-more-part-2.

Karas, Matty. "Red House Breaks Up, Its Members Scatter." *Asbury Park Press*, May 7, 1993.

Infectious: Arthurs, Aaron P. "NYC Pop Band Ivy Has Unique Pop Sensibility." *Indiana-Penn*, February 1995.

Luersson, John D. "Fountains of Wayne: Bright Future in Sales." *American Songwriter*, July/August 2005. https://americansongwriter. com/fountains-of-wayner-bright-future-in-sales/.

Hoskyns, Barney. "Fountains of Wayne: Mojo Rising." *MOJO*, May 2007.

3. We Got Some Big Things Brewing

Krumper, Michael. "Remembering Adam Schlesinger: A Tribute to a Friend." *Flood*, April 15, 2020. https://floodmagazine.com/76966/ remembering-adam-schlesinger-a-tribute-to-a-friend/.

Tayler, Letta. "Fountains of Wayne Making a Splash." *Newsday* (Suffolk edition), January 24, 1997.

Sutcliffe, Phil. "Bastards. Liars. Pimps. Thieves. Scumsuckers. Perverts . . ." *Q*, August 1997.

Deevoy, Adrian. "Fountains of Wayne: How to Be a Rock Manager for a Day." *Blender*, September 2003. https://www.rocksbackpages.com/ Library/Article/fountains-of-wayne-how-to-be-a-rock-manager-for-a-day.

Lambeth, Sam. "Interview: Fountains of Wayne." *Louder Than War*, April 13, 2016. https://louderthanwar.com/interview-fountains-wayne/.

Sprague, David. "Fountains of Wayne Bubble Forth from Scratchie/

Tag." *Billboard*, August 31, 1996.

Howe, Bryan. "Dan Bryk's Misadventures in the Music Industry as Told by Wikipedia." *Indy Week*, April 14, 2020.

"Pink Pop Festival—Fountains of Wayne." YouTube video, posted May 19, 2018. https://www.youtube.com/watch?v=YfW4sTyHlsM.

Luerssen, John D. "Fountains of Wayne: Bright Future in Sales." *American Songwriter*, July/August 2005. https://americansongwriter.com/fountains-of-wayner-bright-future-in-sales/.

Opipari, Ben. "Chris Collingwood, Fountains of Wayne." *Songwriters on Process*, July 25, 2011. https://www.songwritersonprocess.com/blog/2011/07/25/chris-collingwood-fountains-of-wayne.

Klein, Joshua. "Q/A: Adam Schlesinger, Fountains of Wayne Lead Singer." *Argus Leader*, July 5, 2007.

Bray, Ryan. "Fountains of Wayne's Adam Schlesinger Looks Back at 'That Thing You Do!,'" *Consequence of Sound*, September 25, 2016. https://consequence.net/2016/09/fountains-of-waynes-adam-schlesinger-looks-back-on-that-thing-you-do.

Lefton, Clara. "Chris Collingwood: Relishing Musical Connections." *Daily Hampshire Gazette*, October 9, 2010.

Robbins, Ira. "Fountains of Wayne Bubble with Power Pop." *Rolling Stone*, November 28, 1996. https://www.rocksbackpages.com/Library/Article/fountains-of-wayne-bubble-with-power-pop.

Planer, Lindsay. "From Fountains of Wayne Springs Pop Eternal." *Charlotte Observer*, November 20, 1996.

"Celebrating the Legacy of Power Pop." *Times-News*, June 27, 1997.

Cafarelli, Carl. "The History of Power Pop." In Borack, John M. (ed.), *Shake Some Action: The Ultimate Power Pop Guide*. Fort Collins, CO: Not Lame Recording Company, 2007.

"Music for Underdogs." *Chicago Tribune*, December 20, 1996.

Pepper, Tracy. "Fountains of Wayne Play Pop to Ward Off Grunge."

New York Observer, January 1997. https://traceypepper.com/past-writing/journalism/fountains-of-wayne/.

Bellinghausen, Pat. "Concert Tickets Ready—but Are the Pumpkins?" *Billings Gazette*, December 6, 1996.

Simons, Ted. "Wayne's World." *Phoenix New Times*, May 1, 1997. https://www.phoenixnewtimes.com/music/waynes-world-6423163.

Porter, Jody. "Fountains of Wayne Guitarist Jody Porter—New Solo LP." Kickstarter.com, June 24, 2013. https://www.kickstarter.com/projects/jodyporter/month-of-mondays-solo-lp-loud-edgy-with-a-bit-o-ra/description.

Fairey, Shepard. "Month of Mondays / Jody Porter." Obeygiant.com, May 22, 2014. https://obeygiant.com/month-of-mondays-jody-porter/.

Farrar, Steve. "All Set to Ring the Changes!" *Herts and Essex Observer*, June 18, 1992.

Maffei, Ryan. "At Every Speed: An Interview with Jody Porter." *Rock and Roll Globe*, September 4, 2023. https://rockandrollglobe.com/rock/at-every-speed-an-interview-with-jody-porter/.

Catlin, Roger. "Fountains Wail; Murray's in Jail; Shocked Hits Trail." *Hartford Courant*, January 16, 1997.

4. I'm on My Way

Paltrowitz, Darren, host. Interview with Jody Porter. *Paltrocast* (podcast), November 17, 2020. https://www.youtube.com/watch?v=ZIVE9p_4zsk.

Salvo, Jennifer. "Second Fiddle with Big Aspirations." *The Record*, January 24, 1997.

Pettit, John. "Maybe The Pumpkins Need Some Respite from Grind of Touring." *Record Journal*, January 28, 1997.

Spevak, Jeff. "How Can They Stand It?" *Democrat and Chronicle*, January 23, 1997.

Weeks, Janet. "Adam Schlesinger's 'Wonder'-ful year." *Stuart News*, March 14, 1997.

Boehm, Mike. "Worlds of Wayne." *Los Angeles Times*, July 26, 1999.

Ruggieri, Melissa. "Schlesinger's Success Is Not Wayne-Ing." *Richmond Times-Dispatch*, January 2, 1997.

Llewellyn Smith, Caspar. "The Two-Minute Interview." *Daily Telegraph*, May 24, 1997.

Sullivan, Jim. "Fountains of Wayne Offers Pop with an IQ." *Boston Globe*, April 17, 1997.

Sherr, Sara. "Fountains of Wayne Brings Its '60s Style to TLA." *Philadelphia Inquirer*, April 14, 1997.

Ingrassia, Michelle. "Fountains Flow in Philadelphia." *Press Journal*, April 30, 1997.

McCready, John. "Fountains of Wayne: Manchester University." *The Independent*, June 6, 1997.

Pareles, Jon. "Overcoming Life's Slings and Arrows with a Song." *New York Times*, April 19, 1997.

"The Two-Minute Interview." *Daily Telegraph*, May 24, 1997.

EastWest Records, "Big EA&RS???" *The Guardian*, July 12, 1997.

Derdeyn, Stuart. "Sarah McLachlan Launches 30th Anniversary of Fumbling Toward Ecstasy Tour in Vancouver." *Vancouver Sun*, May 18, 2024.

5. So Now Do You Want Me?
Strauss, Neil. "Swirl 360 Twists Synthetic Band Idea." *Indianapolis Star*, June 27, 1998.

Time for a change: Boucher, Christopher. "Making a Splash in Northampton." *Daily Hampshire Gazette*, March 30, 1999.

DeMarco, Jerry. "Ivy Ready to Grow: New Record Company and a Maturing Sound." *The Record*, June 12, 1998.

Gidley, Lisa. "'Utopia' Bubbles Up from Fountains." *Billboard*, March 20, 1999.

Darnell, Steve. "First Person: Chris Collingwood." *Chicago Tribune*, July 9, 1999.

Casimir, Jon. "It's Pop with Both Snap and Crackle." *Sydney Morning Herald*, September 29, 1999.

Cotter, Kelly-Jane. "Paradise Along the Parkway." *Asbury Park Press*, April 2, 1999.

Smith Brady, Lois. "Vows: Katherine Michel, Adam Schlesinger." *New York Times*, February 14, 1999.

Wolliver, Robbie. "A Band Turns Three-Minute Ditties into Paeans to Suburbia." *New York Times*, June 25, 2000.

Attfield, Mike. "Worlds of Wayne." *Los Angeles Times*, July 26, 1999.

Perry, Jonathan. "Fountains of Wayne: Utopia Parkway." *Boston Globe*, April 29, 1999.

McCollum, Brian. "Fountains of Wayne: Utopia Parkway." *Detroit Free Press*, April 18, 1999.

Jezierny, Nick. "Fountains Pour on the Pop." *El Paso Times*, May 1, 1999.

"Fountains of Wayne: Utopia Parkway." *Richmond Times-Dispatch*, May 13, 1999.

Fallon, Scott. "Fountains of Wayne: A Store, a Band: An Unlikely Combo That Really Rocks." *The Record*, June 10, 1999.

Condran, Ed. "Fountains Spring Forth." *The Record*, May 21, 1999.

Weinstein, Ken. "Guest Column: Long-Time Fountains of Wayne Publicist Ken Weinstein Remembers Adam Schlesinger." *RIFF*, April 9, 2020. https://riffmagazine.com/opinion/fountains-of-wayne-publicist-ken-weinstein-adam-schlesinger/.

Catlin, Roger. "Local Flavor Flows Through Fountains' Pop." *Hartford Courant*, May 20, 1999.

Guzmán, Isaac. "Singing the Lives of Average Teen Guys." *Newsday*,

November 11, 1999.

Breithaupt, Don, and Jeff Breithaupt. "Pop from the Fringes." *National Post*, July 3, 1999.

Valania, Jonathan. "Fountains of Wayne at the Troc." *Philadelphia Inquirer*, June 7, 1999.

Kulash, Damian. "Answer Me." *CMJ New Music Monthly*, January 2003.

"Hope Springs Eternal with Fountains of Wayne." *Reading Evening Post*, April 16, 1999.

Walker, Dave. "The Best Band You've Never Heard." *Arizona Republic*, November 7, 1999.

Makin, Robert. "Make Way for the Power Pop Explosion." *Courier-News*, July 8, 1999.

Bumgardner, Ed. "Wayne Manor." *Winston-Salem Journal*, May 21, 1999.

Callahan, Jody. "Pop Crafters Are Unlikely Hitmakers." *Commercial Appeal*, November 21, 2003.

6. Getting Tired of the Twists and Turns

Maestri, Cathy. "Fountains of Wayne Earn Pop Hosannas." *St. Lucie News-Tribune*, August 1, 2003.

Jacobs, Jay S. "Fountains of Wayne: Bright Future in Record Sales." PopEntertainment.com, January 9, 2004. http://www.popentertainment.com/fountains.htm.

Callahan, Jody. "Pop Crafters Are Unlikely Hitmakers." *Commercial Appeal*, November 21, 2003.

Lindquist, David. "Hangover Café Serves Fresh Music and Off-Kilter Wit." *Indianapolis Star,* February 15, 2000.

Gunderson, Edna. "Captain Fantastic's Advice for a Long, Healthy Career." *Press and Sun-Bulletin*, April 5, 2000.

Cohen, Carly. "Fountains of Wayne Perform at Earle." *Asbury Park Press*,

July 11, 2000.

Jordan, Chris. "Interstate." *Central New Jersey Home News*, June 13, 2003.

Moon, Tom. "Who Wrote That Song? Just About Everyone." *Philadelphia Inquirer*, April 3, 2001.

Maiuri, Kevin. "Pop's Fountains Flow in Iron Horse Show." *Daily Hampshire Gazette*, July 12, 2001.

O'Brien, Conan. "Conan Remembers Adam Schlesinger & A Very Special Fountains of Wayne Performance." Team Coco YouTube channel, April 2, 2020. https://www.youtube.com/watch?v=jTNonlossl0.

Stein, Joel. "How I Nearly Killed VH1." *Time*, February 2, 2004. https://time.com/archive/6928044/how-i-nearly-killed-vh1/.

Pacienza, Angela. "No Celebrity Is Sacred in New Animated Series." *Sault Star*, June 4, 2003.

Louie, Rebecca. "Fountains of Wayne Plays It Cool." (New York) *Daily News*, July 8, 2003.

Luerssen, John D. "Fountains of Wayne: Bright Future in Sales." *American Songwriter*, July/August 2005. https://americansongwriter.com/fountains-of-wayner-bright-future-in-sales/.

Lauden, S. W. "'Welcome Interstate Managers' Turns 20." *Big Takeover*, September 21, 2023. https://bigtakeover.com/essays/welcome-interstate-managers-turns-20.

Anderman, Joan. "Mike Denneen: His Keen Ear, Instincts Guided Musicians." *Boston Globe*, July 19, 2018.

Morris, Chris. "Fountains of Wayne Celebrates Biz World." *Billboard*, June 14, 2003.

Haymes, Greg. "Fountains of Wayne Flowing Smoothly." *Johnson City Press*, July 19, 2004.

Condran, Ed. "Embarking on a Voyage of Discovery." *The Record*,

November 1, 2002.

7. Got It Goin' On

Deevoy, Adrian. "Fountains of Wayne: How to Be a Rock Manager for a Day." *Blender*, September 2003. https://www.rocksbackpages.com/Library/Article/fountains-of-wayne-how-to-be-a-rock-manager-for-a-day.

Muther, Christopher. "That Thing He Does: A Chat with Mike Viola." *Boston Globe*, August 19, 2004.

McCollum, Brian. "Cartoon Among Projects for Fountains of Wayne." *Detroit Free Press*, November 13, 2002.

Condran, Ed. "Waxing and Wayne-ing." *Asbury Park Press*, November 2, 2002.

Klein, Joshua. "Power-Pop Hooks, Clever Lyrics Give Fountains an Edge." *Chicago Tribune*, November 18, 2002.

Appelbaum, Alec. "60 Seconds with Adam Schlesinger." *Fast Company*, December 1, 2003. https://www.fastcompany.com/47853/60-seconds-adam-schlesinger.

Fulks, Robbie. "Here's How Adam Schlesinger Did That Thing He Did." Talkhouse.com, April 8, 2020. https://www.talkhouse.com/heres-how-adam-schlesinger-did-that-thing-he-did/.

Sperounes, Sandra. "Obscurity to Absurdity." *Edmonton Journal*, December 21, 2003.

Me & Julio: Maffei, Ryan. "At Every Speed: An Interview with Jody Porter." *Rock and Roll Globe,* September 4, 2023. https://rockandrollglobe.com/rock/at-every-speed-an-interview-with-jody-porter/.

Youngs, Whitney. "Fountains of Disenchantment." *Daily Breeze*, May 26, 2004. https://www.dailybreeze.com/2004/05/26/fountains-of-disenchantment-5-27/.

Boatwright, David. "Back to the Baystate, Northampton MA." *Live Music News and Reviews*, March 10, 2010. https://livemusicnewsandreview.com/2020/03/academy-of-music/.

Beckerman, Jim. "The Soundtrack of Hackensack." *The Record*, July 8, 2003.

Anderman, Joan. "After a Decade of Guitar Fuzz, the Keyboard Is King Again." *Boston Globe*, February 20, 2005.

Kielty, Tom. "CD Report: Fountains of Wayne, Welcome Interstate Managers." *Boston Globe*, June 13, 2003.

Moeller, Sean. "CD Reviews: Welcome Interstate Managers, Fountains of Wayne." *Quad-City Times*, May 29, 2003.

Gamboa, Glenn. "Wayne's World Unearths Glee amid Gloom." *Newsday*, May 11, 2004.

Infectious: Paiva, Derek. "10 Best Albums of 2003." *Honolulu Star-Advertiser*, December 29, 2003.

Kot, Greg. "'Stacy's Mom' Just One Part of Wayne Puzzle." *Chicago Tribune*, November 21, 2003. https://www.chicagotribune.com/news/ct-xpm-2003-11-21-0311210299-story.html.

Griffin, Andrew. "Fountains of Wayne Crank Out a Whiner." *Town Talk*, July 26, 2003.

Kenyon, John. "Fountains' Tunes Mix Smoothly." *The Gazette*, July 31, 2003.

Wawzenek, Bryan. "Just Asking: A Conversation with Adam Schlesinger of Fountains of Wayne." *Northwest Herald*, December 23, 2005.

Al Teller, quoted in Tannenbaum, Rob, and Craig Marks. *I Want My MTV: The Uncensored Story of the Music Video Revolution*. New York: Plume/Penguin Books, 2012.

Powills, Nick. "Say What??: Chattin' It Up with Adam Schlesinger." *Northwest Herald*, November 14, 2003.

Kimes, Ken. "Clinic's for More than Drummers." *Sun News*, April 23, 2004.

Page, Jeffrey. "Road to Jersey's Heart." *The Record*, May 23, 2004.

FOUNTAINS OF WAYNE

Daley, David. "Happy to Be Nominated. Really." *Journal News*, February 5, 2004.

Gunderson, Edna. "Downloading Threatens to Put the Album in Its Grave." *Leaf-Chronicle*, December 5, 2003.

Guarino, Mark. "Nada Surf." *Daily Herald*, April 4, 2008.

Kleinman, David. "Fountains of Wayne Perform Songs from Newest Release at Sellersville." *The Mercury*, March 6, 2013.

Bray, Ryan. "Fountains of Wayne's Adam Schlesinger Looks Back at 'That Thing You Do!'" *Consequence of Sound*, September 25, 2016. https://consequence.net/2016/09/fountains-of-waynes-adam-schlesinger-looks-back-on-that-thing-you-do.

Carr, David. "Hot Off the Turnpike, a New Cool." *New York Times*, August 3, 2003.

Carpenter, Susan. "Making a Big Splash—Again." *Los Angeles Times*, May 14, 2004.

Kloer, Phil. "Christian Band Converts Rock Hits and Rap." *Atlanta Constitution*, December 9, 2004.

"What's the Best Rock Song Ever?" *Des Moines Register*, January 23, 2005.

Van Vleck, Philip. "'Regular Guys' Headline Show at ESA." *Herald-Sun*, April 13, 2003.

Luersson, John D. "Fountains of Wayne: Bright Future in Sales." *American Songwriter*, July/August 2005. https://americansongwriter.com/fountains-of-wayner-bright-future-in-sales/.

Brothers, Michael A. "Matchbox Twenty." *Springfield News-Leader*, November 13, 2003.

Rice, Jeff. "The Lowdown: Man Behind the BJC Magic." *Centre Daily Times*, October 27, 2003.

Mansfield, Brian. "Rob Thomas Headed for 'Great Unknown' Tour." *Daily Times*, June 11, 2015.

Jacobs, Jay S. "Fountains of Wayne: Bright Future in Record Sales." PopEntertainment.com, January 9, 2004. http://www.popentertainment.com/fountains.htm.

Morse, Steve. "Hip-Hop Shakes Up Grammy Nominations." *Boston Globe*, December 3, 2003.

McGinn, Andrew. "Describing the Indescribable." *Springfield News-Sun*, December 11, 2003.

Moon, Tom. "Time for Grammys to Put Outkast Out Front." *Philadelphia Inquirer*, February 8, 2004.

8. A Strange and Foreign Place
Carpenter, Susan. "Making a Big Splash—Again." *Los Angeles Times*, May 13, 2004.

Cooper, Peter. "'Stacy's Mom' Band Funny, Poignant." *The Tennessean*, May 1, 2004.

Jacobs, Jay S. "Fountains of Wayne: Bright Future in Record Sales." PopEntertainment.com, January 9, 2004. http://www.popentertainment.com/fountains.htm.

Adamson, April. "Hot Threads and Lots to Dread." *Philadelphia Daily News*, February 9, 2004.

Luersson, John D. "Fountains of Wayne: Bright Future in Sales." *American Songwriter*, July/August 2005. https://americansongwriter.com/fountains-of-wayner-bright-future-in-sales/.

Piccoli, Sean. "Bright Future." *South Florida Sun Sentinel*, April 24, 2004.

Hamfeldt, Rebecca. "Fountains of Wayne Draws on N.J. Roots." *Daily Record*, April 23, 2004.

Cheal, David. "On the Powerpop Button." *Daily Telegraph*, March 5, 2004.

Senft, Michael. "Foremost Thrill." *Arizona Republic*, January 29, 2004.

Harkness, Geoff. "Full 'Plates.'" *Chicago Tribune*, July 12, 2005.

Cormier, Ryan. "We Do Dewey, Don't We?" *News Journal*, June 4, 2004.

Buckner, Brent. "Giving the People What They Want." *Anniston Star*, June 17, 2004.

DeLuca, Dan. "The Fulfillment Was Not Total." *Philadelphia Inquirer*, June 30, 2004.

"Ivy: A Tribute to Adam Schlesinger." Ivy Official YouTube channel. Posted October 19, 2021. https://www.youtube.com/watch?v=w8xISJVl4lQ.

Wynn Rousuck, J. "'Cry-Baby' on Broadway Selects Songwriting Team." *Baltimore Sun*, March 19, 2004.

Rabin, Nathan. "Adam Schlesinger." The A.V. Club, April 25, 2007. https://www.avclub.com/adam-schlesinger-1798211299.

9. Looking for a New Routine

Muther, Christopher. "Pop Pick: Ivy." *Boston Globe*, April 25, 2005.

Luersson, John D. "Fountains of Wayne: Bright Future in Sales." *American Songwriter,* July/August 2005. https://americansongwriter.com/fountains-of-wayner-bright-future-in-sales/.

Fulks, Robbie. "Adam Schlesinger Celebrated by 'Fountains of Wayne Hotline' Creator Robbie Fulks." *Variety*, April 2, 2020. https://variety.com/2020/music/news/adam-schlesinger-celebrated-fountains-of-wayne-hotline-robbie-fulks-1234569967/.

Youngs, Stuart. "Great Scott! Fountains of Wayne Tap Montclair Connection for Album Track." *Montclair Times*, October 27, 2005.

Maroon, Annie. "CD Review: Out-of-State Plates." *Pittsburgh Post-Gazette*, September 17, 2005.

Luerssen, John D. "Fountains of Wayne: Bright Future in Sales." *American Songwriter*, July/August 2005. https://americansongwriter.com/fountains-of-wayner-bright-future-in-sales/.

Abebe, Nitsuh. "Whatever: The '90s Box Set." *Pitchfork*, July 24, 2005. https://pitchfork.com/reviews/albums/1971-whatever-the-90s-box-set/.

Wazwanek, Bryan. "Just Asking: A Conversation with Adam Schlesinger of Fountains of Wayne." *Northwest Herald*, December 23, 2005.

"Fountains of Wayne Gets Back to the Studio." *Fresno Bee*, January 20, 2006.

Holahan, Catherine. "Songwriter Splits His Time and Talent Between Distinct Pop Bands." *The Record*, January 30, 2006.

Wasser, Chris. "Wayne's World." *Irish Independent*, October 29, 2011.

Lanham, Tom. "Fountains of Wayne Frontman Keeps It Goin' On." *San Francisco Examiner*, April 30, 2007.

Shanahan, Mark. "For Fountains of Wayne Singer, a Liberating New Musical Landscape." *Boston Globe*, May 26, 2019.

Rodman, Sarah. "They've Got a Lot Going On." *Boston Globe*, July 30, 2011.

Graff, Gary. "Sunny 'Weather': Fountains of Wayne Follows Breakthrough Hit with Hook-Heavy New Disc." *Billboard*, April 21, 2007.

Paltrowitz, Darren (host). Interview with Jody Porter. *Paltrocast* (podcast), November 17, 2020. https://www.youtube.com/watch?v=ZIVE9p_4zsk.

"America." *Central New Jersey Home News*, May 20, 2006.

Rabin, Nathan. "Adam Schlesinger." The A.V. Club, April 25, 2007. https://www.avclub.com/adam-schlesinger-1798211299.

Simons, Dave. "Tips from the Top: Chris Collingwood of Fountains of Wayne." BMI.com, July 2, 2007. https://www.bmi.com/news/entry/Tips_from_the_Top_Chris_Collingwood_of_Fountains_of_Wayne.

Maffei, Ryan. "At Every Speed: An Interview with Jody Porter." *Rock and Roll Globe*, September 4, 2023. https://rockandrollglobe.com/rock/at-every-speed-an-interview-with-jody-porter/.

Hunter, Sheryl. "Fountains of Wayne Goes with the Flow." *The Recorder*, April 19, 2007.

FOUNTAINS OF WAYNE

Graff, Gary. "Sunny 'Weather': Fountains of Wayne Follows Breakthrough Hit with Hook-Heavy New Disc." *Billboard*, April 21, 2007.

Poniewozik, James. "Officeworkers Need a Springsteen Too." *Time*, May 28, 2007.

Danton, Eric R. "Everyday Songs for a Rush Hour Culture." *Hartford Courant*, April 5, 2007.

Bauder, David. "Fountains of Wayne Are Back with Detailed Tales of Suburban Lives." *Lancaster Eagle-Gazette*, April 1, 2007.

McCollum, Brian. "Fountains of Wayne: Traffic and Weather." *Detroit Free Press*, April 1, 2007.

Mervis, Scott. "Fountains Flowing." *Pittsburgh Post-Gazette*, June 7, 2007.

Cormier, Ryan. "Stacy's Mom Comes to Philly." *News Journal*, May 4, 2007.

Rodman, Sarah. "Plenty of Bubbly Pop from Fountains of Wayne." *Boston Globe*, April 24, 2007.

Robbins, Ira. "Reason to Gush over Fountains." *Newsday*, April 27, 2007.

Q104.3 radio (New York) interview with Adam Schlesinger, January 8, 2008.

"By the Numbers." *Los Angeles Times*, April 2, 2007.

Gottlieb, Steven. "In Depth: Fountains of Wayne's 'Someone to Love.'" Videostatic, May 4, 2007. https://www.videostatic.com/content/depth-fountains-wayne-someone-love.

McCauley, Mary Carole. "Waters' Next Act." *Baltimore Sun*, November 18, 2007.

Mervis, Scott. "Fountains Flowing." *Pittsburgh Post-Gazette*, June 7, 2007.

Hunter, Sheryl. "Fountains of Wayne Goes with the Flow." *The Recorder*, April 19, 2007.

10. Just You Wait
McCauley, Mary Carole. "Cry-Baby Has Flash, Wit, but No Heart." *Baltimore Sun*, May 8, 2008.

Robertson, Campbell. "Roads to Recognition That Were Really Short." *New York Times*, June 6, 2008. https://www.nytimes.com/2008/06/01/theater/theaterspecial/01debu. html.

Coyle, Jake. "Hark! The Herald Colbert in HIS Christmas Special." *South Bend Tribune*, November 21, 2008.

Maiuri, Ken. "Rivet-Popping Songs." *Daily Hampshire Gazette*, June 5, 2008.

"Out of the Shadows, into the Light: An Interview with Jody Porter." PopMatters.com, September 14, 2010. https://www.popmatters. com/130729-out-of-the-shadows-into-the-light-an-interview-with-jody-porter-2496141124.html.

Carter, Bill. "Colbert: Christmas' Champion" (*New York Times* Syndicate). *Johnson City Press*, November 22, 2008.

Ayers, Michael. "Fountains Working on Fresh Tunes" (Billboard.com News Service). *The Record*, November 26, 2008.

Groce, Larry. Interview with Adam Schlesinger and Chris Collingwood for NPR Mountain Stage, March 2009. https://www.youtube.com/watch?v=2GywwxZtIDU.

Danton, Eric R. "Acoustic Fountains of Wayne Still Pack a Wallop." *Hartford Courant*, March 3, 2009.

Adams, Sam. "Fountains Unplugs the Irony." *Philadelphia Inquirer*, February 23, 2009.

Ragogna, Mike. "A Conversation with Fountains of Wayne." *Huffington Post*, August 1, 2011.

Graff, Gary. "Tinted Windows" (*New York Times Syndicate*). *Edmonton*

Journal, June 7, 2009.

Sun-Times Wire. "SWSX 2009, Night Three: Tinted Windows, Superdrag, and Graham Coxon." *Chicago Sun-Times*, March 20, 2009. https://chicago.suntimes.com/news/2009/3/20/18615337/sxsw-2009-night-three-tinted-windows-superdrag-amp-graham-coxon.

Verdon, Joan. "Landmark Store's Fate Uncertain." *The Record*, March 14, 2009.

Lipkin, Gregg. "All the Things They Do: A Superstar Interview with Mike Viola and Adam Schlesinger." PopMatters, July 26, 2010. https://www.popmatters.com/128718-all-the-things-they-do-2496163457.html.

Groce, Larry. Interview for NPR Mountain Stage, March 2009. https://www.youtube.com/watch?v=2GywwxZtIDU.

Columbia Law School Public Affairs Office. "Paying Dues: A Fact of Life for Both Musicians and Their Lawyers." November 18, 2009. https://www.law.columbia.edu/news/archive/paying-dues-fact-life-both-musicians-and-their-lawyers.

"Chris Collingwood Interview." Boston.com, July 29, 2011.

11. Another State of Mind
"A Serious Dude." Wirenh.com, August 25, 2011. https://chriscollingwoodfanclub.wordpress.com/2011/08/25/wirenh-com-interview-with-chris-collingwood/.

Goudreau, Chris. "Famed Musician Dies at 52." *Valley Advocate*, April 9, 2020.

Rodman, Sarah. "They've Got a Lot Going On." *Boston Globe*, July 30, 2011.

Shanahan, Mark. "For Fountains of Wayne Singer, a Liberating New Musical Landscape." *Boston Globe*, May 23, 2019.

Downing, Andy. "Fountains Get a Bit Serious on New Album." *Capital Times*, April 26, 2012.

Knopper, Steve. "Overflowing with Power Pop." *Newsday*, May 11, 2012.

Wasser, Chris. "Wayne's World." *Irish Independent*, October 29, 2011.

"Ivy: A Tribute to Adam Schlesinger." Ivy Official YouTube channel. Posted October 19, 2021. https://www.youtube.com/watch?v=w8xISJVl4lQ.

Biese, Alex. "Only in America: Fountains of Wayne Get Scooped on Their Own Material." *Central New Jersey Home News*, July 22, 2011.

Beckerman, Jim. "Fountains of Wayne Ends the Drought." *The Record*, July 21, 2011.

Raftery, Brian. "Denizens of the Quotidien." *New York*, July 8, 2011. https://nymag.com/arts/popmusic/features/fountains-of-wayne-2011-7/.

Morrison, Jim. "Life after Fountains of Wayne." *Veer*, October 2011. https://veermag.com/2016/10/life-after-fountains-of-wayne/.

Maffei, Ryan. "At Every Speed: An Interview with Jody Porter." *Rock and Roll Globe*, September 4, 2023. https://rockandrollglobe.com/rock/at-every-speed-an-interview-with-jody-porter/.

Triplett, Gene. "Hanson to 'Shout It Out' in Tulsa." *Daily Oklahoman*, August 20, 2010.

Lefton, Clara. "Chris Collingwood: Relishing Musical Connections." *Daily Hampshire Gazette*, October 9, 2010.

Yep Roc Records press release, April 11, 2011. https://www.yeproc.com/fountains-of-wayne-sign-to-yep-roc-new-album-sky-full-of-holes-available-82-2/.

Yep Roc Records. "YR15: About Yep Roc Records." January 1, 2012. https://www.yeproc.com/yr15-about-yep-roc-records/.

"Lori Nix and Kathleen Gerber." https://www.artworksforchange.org/portfolio/lori-nix/.

Opipari, Ben. "Chris Collingwood, Fountains of Wayne." Songwriters on Process, July 25, 2011. https://www.songwritersonprocess.com/blog/2011/07/25/chris-collingwood-fountains-of-wayne.

Chimento, Matt. "Fountains of Wayne's Style Bridges CD to MP3."

Courier-Post, August 5, 2011.

Block, Melissa. "Fountains of Wayne: Transcending Time and Place." *All Things Considered*, NPR Radio, September 21, 2011. https://www.npr.org/transcripts/140664307.

Hyden, Steven. "Growing Up: A Great Power-Pop Band Stares Down Middle Age." *Chicago Tribune*, August 4, 2011.

Farber, Jim. "Wayne Manner: Pop Portraits." *New York Daily News*, August 9, 2011.

Hirsh, Marc. "Fountains of Wayne: Sky Full of Holes." *Boston Globe*, August 2, 2011.

Triplett, Gene. "Group Candy Golde Mines Rich Vein." *Daily Oklahoman*, May 13, 2011.

Lanham, Tom. "MMM Hanson!" *San Francisco Examiner*, September 6, 2011.

Brasor, Philip. "Fountains of Wayne Play to the Choir."

PhilipBrasor.com, March 31, 2012. https://philipbrasor.com/2012/03/31/fountains-of-wayne-play-to-the-choir/.

Graff, Gary. "Fountains of Wayne's Schlesinger: 'There's Interest' in New Tinted Windows Music." *Billboard*, March 3, 2012. https://www.billboard.com/music/music-news/fountains-of-waynes-schlesinger-theres-interest-in-new-tinted-windows-music-489151/.

Farber, Jim. "The Wayne Manner of Pop." *New York Daily News*, April 19, 2012.

Vogt, Tiffany. "Wedding Band: Musician Adam Schlesinger Interview." *TV Watchtower*, December 1, 2012. https://thetvwatchtower.org/2012/12/01/musician-adam-schlesinger-talks-about-bringing-the-cool-music-of-tbs-new-comedy-series-wedding-band-to-life/.

12. Evolve in Time
Aberbach, Brian. "After Four Long Years, Fountains of Wayne Lets the Music Flow." *Herald-News*, March 12, 2013.

Ruiz, Lorena. "Children's Author Boynton: 'I Think of Myself as Mostly Writing for People.'" NBCNews.com, September 9, 2013. https://www.nbcnews.com/id/wbna52961347.

McCall, Tris. "Songwriter Helps Out with Online Comedy." *The Record*, May 13, 2013.

Porter, Jody. "Fountains of Wayne Guitarist Jody Porter—New Solo LP." Kickstarter.com, June 24, 2013. https://www.kickstarter.com/projects/jodyporter/month-of-mondays-solo-lp-loud-edgy-with-a-bit-o-ra/description.

Krumper, Michael. "Remembering Adam Schlesinger: A Tribute to a Friend." *Flood*, April 15, 2020. https://floodmagazine.com/76966/remembering-adam-schlesinger-a-tribute-to-a-friend/.

Shanahan, Mark. "For Fountains of Wayne Singer, a Liberating New Musical Landscape." *Boston Globe*, May 26, 2019.

Keveney, Bill. "Song, Dance Fuel Bloom's 'Crazy' CW Adventure." *Green Bay Press-Gazette*, October 10, 2015.

Fernandez, Maria Elena. "'He Was the Music': Remembering Adam Schlesinger with the Creators, Songwriters, and Cast of 'Crazy Ex-Girlfriend.'" *Vulture*, April 3, 2020. https://www.vulture.com/2020/04/adam-schlesinger-crazy-ex-girlfriend-music-remembrance.html.

Lambeth, Sam. "Interview: Fountains of Wayne." *Louder Than War*, April 13, 2016. https://louderthanwar.com/interview-fountains-wayne/.

"Look Park" press release. Missing Piece Group, April 2016. https://www.missingpiecegroup.com/look-park.

Lewis, Randy. "At 50, Monkees Have New Album" (*Los Angeles Times* news service). *Merced Sun-Star*, May 21, 2016.

13. Unwelcome Fate

VanHoose, Benjamin. "Adam Schlesinger's Girlfriend Shares Last Photo Taken Before His Death: 'I Love You So, So Much'" (quotes in story from posts on Instagram account @alexismorley). *People*, April 27, 2020. https://people.com/music/adam-schlesinger-girlfriend-shares-last-photo-taken-together/.

Biese, Alex. "Adam Schlesinger of Fountains of Wayne Hospitalized in NY." Montclair Times, April 2, 2020.

COVID-19 mortality rates: Our World of Data, for week ending April 6, 2020. *https://ourw*orldindata.org/grapher/weekly-covid-deaths?tab=table&time=2020-04-06..latest&region=NorthAmerica.

Freeman, Jeremy. "The Unfathomable Reality of Loss: Adam Schlesinger, 1967–2020." Oishi Gevalt, April 8, 2020. https://oishigevalt.com/2020/04/08/the-unfathomable-reality-of-loss-adam-schlesinger-1967-2020/.

Mallenbaum, Carly. "Tom Hanks Remembers 'That Thing You Do!' Songwriter Adam Schlesinger: 'He Was a One-Der.'" *USA Today*, April 1, 2020. https://www.usatoday.com/story/entertainment/music/2020/04/01/adam-schlesinger-coronavirus-tom-hanks-twitter-reaction/5109790002/.

Romano, Nick. "Rachel Bloom on the Death of *Crazy Ex-Girlfriend*'s Adam Schlesinger: 'He Is Irreplaceable.'" *Entertainment Weekly,* April 2, 2020. https://ew.com/tv/adam-schlesinger-dead-rachel-bloom-crazy-ex-girlfriend/.

Vozick-Levinson, Simon. "Fountains of Wayne's Chris Collingwood Remembers Adam Schlesinger, His Friend and Bandmate." *Rolling Stone*, April 10, 2020. https://www.rollingstone.com/music/music-features/adam-schlesinger-fountains-of-wayne-chris-collingwood-980798/.

Maffei, Ryan. "At Every Speed: An Interview with Jody Porter." *Rock and Roll Globe*, September 4, 2023. https://rockandrollglobe.com/rock/at-every-speed-an-interview-with-jody-porter/.

Stairiker, Kevin. "'Stacy's Mom' Guitarist Jody Porter to Rock Tellus 360 with Free Show Saturday Night." LNP Always Lancaster, July 29, 2021. https://lancasteronline.com/features/entertainment/stacys-mom-guitarist-jody-porter-to-rock-tellus360-with-free-show-saturday-interview/article_03465b44-efd0-11eb-8ec7-cbdc53a47cf6.html.

Epilogue: Shine On, Shine On, Shine On
Krumper, Michael. "Remembering Adam Schlesinger: A Tribute to a Friend." *Flood*, April 15, 2020. https://floodmagazine.com/76966/remembering-adam-schlesinger-a-tribute-to-a-friend/.

Weinstein, Ken. "Guest Column: Long-Time Fountains of Wayne Publicist Ken Weinstein Remembers Adam Schlesinger." *RIFF*, April 9, 2020. https://riffmagazine.com/opinion/fountains-of-wayne-publicist-ken-weinstein-adam-schlesinger/.

Burr, Ty. "Schlesinger's Gifts to Us: Fountains of Wayne and Songcraft." *Boston Globe*, April 3, 2020.

Rosen, Jody. "Adam Schlesinger's Incandescent Songwriting Talent." *New Yorker*, April 3, 2020. https://www.newyorker.com/culture/postscript/adam-schlesingers-incandescent-songwriting-talent.

Snyder, Elizabeth. "Coronavirus Hits This Fan in the Gut." *Kenosha News*, April 8, 2020.

Gehrett, Les. "Furlough, Death, and Music." *Lebanon Express*, April 29, 2020.

www.ingramcontent.com/pod-product-compliance
Lightning Source LLC
Chambersburg PA
CBHW021152130626
46554CB00005B/1783